THE HEIST
OF THE CENTURY...

In the spring of 1873 four young Americans challenged the Bank of England and almost got away with £100,000. The caper created an international scandal. The culprits were George Bidwell, mastermind of the plot; his brother Austin, the front man; George Macdonnell, an expert at forgery; and a fourth man, who later joined the scheme.

Amid the headlines and the sensation the ingenious scoundrels escaped London and led their pursuers on a frantic chase halfway across Europe. With a supporting cast of beautiful, willing ladies and the cleverest detectives Scotland Yard could offer, this is an edge-of-your-seat suspense story that will keep the reader enthralled to its shocking climax.

ANN HUXLEY
FOUR AGAINST THE BANK OF ENGLAND

PLAYBOY
PAPERBACKS

CONTENTS

ILLUSTRATIONS

AUTHOR'S NOTE

The basis of my research for this book was the verbatim report of the trial of the four Americans at the Old Bailey, and many of the conversations have been built up from words remembered by witnesses.

In the British Museum newspaper library I read contemporary reports of the discovery of the fraud, and the chase for the offenders, as well as useful comments on the progress of the trial. All these facts I have incorporated in the story. The papers included *The Times*, the *Daily Telegraph*, the *Evening Standard, the City Press*, the *Illustrated London News*, the *New York Herald Tribune*, the *Cork Examiner* and the *Irish Times*.

I was lucky to discover from America a book published by the Bidwell brothers after their release from prison. Entitled *Forging His Own Chains, or Bidwell's Travels from Wall Street to Newgate*, this volume produced many interesting small scenes, although some of the facts did not tally with official reports of the trial and all reference to George Bidwell's mistress is omitted.

When part of the book appeared in an international magazine a Mrs. Prentice Bassett wrote to me saying that her father, an American post-office official, had traveled to England for the Old Bailey trial. Among his papers Mrs. Bassett discovered the letter which Austin Bidwell wrote to his wife from prison, the text of which I have included.

Most of the books listed in the bibliography and many others I used for background reading I borrowed from the London Library.

1

THE
FUSE IS LIT

The twenty-seven-ton steam engine Lucifer 1004 hurled itself along the railway track cut through the heart of England. Sheep in the rain-drenched fields raised their heads when the smoking monster appeared, but lost their nerve and scattered to the furthest hedge before the last of the twenty-three coaches racketed by. The train was a non-stop express from London to Birmingham and at 1:15 p.m. precisely it steamed into New Street Station.

Directly the seven-foot driving wheels nudged the locomotive against the platform buffers George Bidwell stepped down from the foremost carriage of the train. He crossed the platform, threading his way between porters and empty luggage trolleys, and disappeared through revolving doors leading into the Queen's Hotel.

Bidwell omitted to give his name when he asked for a private sitting-room at the reception desk. But the sharp eyes of the hotel porter who showed him upstairs absorbed his appearance—"a foreign-looking gentleman, with a white silk scarf, and satchel or sort of traveling bag over his shoulder."

Bidwell forestalled this porter as he unlocked the door of Room 18.

"Thank you," he said firmly.

"I will build up the fire, sir."

"I can attend to it myself." Bidwell nodded briefly, stepped into the room and closed the door in the man's face. He pulled off his overcoat and scarf and hung

9

them on the bentwood hatstand. Without a glance at the restrained opulence of the dark paneled room, Bidwell crossed the thick carpet and sat down at the desk. A sheet of blotting paper stared up at him, quill pens and filled inkstand lay close to his right hand. Bidwell swept these aside and drew from his satchel his own writing materials.

George Bidwell was thirty-three, but he looked older. His body was compact and thickset and he was immaculately groomed. He had black hair and a sallow skin, marked with a long crease of intensity between the eyes. His nose was long and dominant, his eyes brown, wide-set but cold. An insignificant lip had been obliterated by a superb Kaiser-type moustache, and his lower lip was red and strong. It was supported by a very square, thrusting chin.

Bidwell examined the only word on the sheet of notepaper in front of him. It was a signature, written boldly two inches from the bottom of the page. He picked up his pen and began to fill in the rest of the letter. The act required intense concentration because Bidwell was not using his own handwriting. The swooping downward loops of the g's and f's, the widely separated words and elegant forward slant of the sentences, were idiosyncrasies of his brother's style.

When it was finished Bidwell blotted the letter carefully and read it through:

Birmingham, January 21st, 1873
Dear Sir,
    I hand you herewith, as per enclosed, memorandum bills for discount, the proceeds of which please place to my credit.

F. A. Warren

The signature followed naturally, and the businesslike and arid phrasing of the note revealed none of the mounting excitement in George Bidwell's mind. Before sealing the envelope he slipped three pieces of paper between the folds of the letter. These were the bills whose explosive properties had lain dormant so long as they remained in Bidwell's possession. Now he was going to post them. He sealed the envelope and addressed it:

> The Bank of England
> Western Branch
> Burlington Gardens,
> Mayfair, London

Before leaving the sitting-room Bidwell tore the used sheet off the blotting pad and threw it into the fire. He went out to find a cab.

The General Post Office was only a short distance from the station but the approaches to New Street were clogged with loaded wagons heaped with such necessities of Victorian life as iron bedsteads, encrusted umbrella stands and children's toys. Birmingham was the boom town of the Midlands. It was crammed with enthusiastic inhabitants proud of their capabilities. They had established small manufacturing businesses in every side-road of the city. The station was the transportation depot for their wares. By the time the cab drew up at the post office it was 2:05 p.m. Bidwell ordered the driver down from his box and sent him to register the letter.

It was mere formality for Bidwell to accept the registration receipt. The cab-driver remembered: "Bidwell folded it, and then, ripping it up into shreds, threw them into the street." Bidwell required no souvenir of the posting. The whole contents of the registered letter were home-made forgeries.

Forgeries! Posted direct to the Bank of England! It was an impertinence without parallel in the records of Threadneedle Street. The Bank of England was immensely rich and influential, the principal bank of deposit and circulation in the world. It was hedged in with security and red tape, and neither veteran confidence tricksters nor the most desperate thieves even considered the bank as a possible victim.

But George Bidwell belonged to a syndicate possessing novel aspirations. Their current project was to rob the Bank of England of £100,000 at a time when the pound was worth many times what it is today.

George Bidwell was American. So were his brother Austin and George Macdonnell. The three men possessed charm, talent and ample funds. The Bidwells, thirty-three and twenty-five years old respectively, were experienced Wall Street operators. George Macdonnell, aged twenty-six, was the Harvard-educated son of an established Boston family. This strikingly attractive trio had landed at Southampton in April 1872 with all the conventional trappings of young Americans beginning the Grand Tour.

When they stepped off the boat train they did not take a cab to Claridges or another of the leading hotels in London. They moved instead to modest lodgings in Haggerstone, a suburb of North London, giving false names to the landlady. During the first days they took things quietly. Wandering through the London streets, visiting historical monuments, gazing into shop windows, and studying passing traffic. At first they were impeded by groups of filthy and emaciated street-vendors. But they grew deaf to their cries and gradually assimilated the casual walk and mannerisms of English men-about-town.

Returning from a steamboat trip up the Thames one evening, the three Americans disembarked from Blackfriars Pier. The last of the day-cabs were straggling home across the river as the Americans, in search of a place to dine, sauntered up through twisting cobbled streets into the deserted City sector.

George Bidwell listened uneasily to his companions' superfluous conversation. They had been in England a week. He was anxious to get down to business. The three men had crossed the Atlantic with the express purpose of "raising the wind out of the capitalists of Europe." It had taken them only a few days to realize that for this purpose it was unnecessary to cross the Channel. England's old enemy, France, was crippled after the disastrous Franco-German war of 1870, and Germany and Italy were each busy working out the complexities of their newly gained national unity.

Britain was enjoying a period of furious industrial activity. Her export trade was at its maximum, and the recent opening of the Suez Canal had swollen her shipping to 1,200,000 tons—exceeding her nearest rival, the U.S.A., by a clear million tons. The heart of her mighty empire was London, and here the Bidwells decided to stay. On the boat each man had contributed £400 to a working fund, and stipulated their partnership should be binding for a year. Practical details of the scheme had been left until they reached the site of operations.

At a road junction the three men paused, wondering which way to turn. George Bidwell glanced up at the street name on the wall. Sharply he turned to his friends.

"This is Lombard Street," he said. They gazed at the dignified buildings, conforming roughly to the Italianate style, with simple columns supporting tripartite windows and elegant roof cornices. This was where the Lombards, from northern Italy, had set up their benches in the open street after the original Jewish money-lenders to the City had been expelled by Edward I in 1280. Macdonnell lifted his top-hat formally.

"Hail Lombard Street," he said. "Financial heart of the Empire."

"This is where we begin," George Bidwell said firmly. The two younger men stared at him a moment, then Macdonnell strode across the road. He touched with his cane the brass inscribed plate on the door ahead.

"No. 52 Lombard Street," he read. "Dreyfus Schroder

and Company, Merchants. London and California Mining Company. Sierra Buttes Gold Mining Company. Take your pick."

The three men turned westward, reading the name plates as they walked.

"No. 40, Morris and Grave, Merchants. L. Bellot, East India Merchant."

"No. 74, Curtis and Harvey, Gunpowder Manufacturers."

"No. 76, Hills Percival, Bankers."

"No. 77, Fuller Banbury and Mathieson, Bankers."

"No. 81, Books and Company, Bankers."

They had reached a huge intersection, the apex of the six most fabulous streets in Britain's long financial history, Princes Street, Poultry, King William Street, Lombard Street, Cornhill and Threadneedle Street. Directly ahead, flickering gaslamps lit up the splendid eight-pillared façade of the Bank of England.

"Boys, you can depend upon it, there is the softest spot in the world," Austin said. "We could hit the bank for a million as easy as rolling off a log."

His companions agreed laughingly. "But right now we need food."

They turned down past the Mansion House, and went into the Cannon Street Hotel for dinner.

In the foyer Austin picked up a book—*Murray's Handbook of Modern London*. He flicked through it.

"How about this?" he asked his friends. "Since 1870 several four-horse stage-coaches have started to run during the spring and summer months to places within easy reach of London; these are conducted and driven by gentlemen, owners of the horses. The appointments are first-rate. The coach to Windsor starts at 1 p.m., through Kew, Hampton Court and Virginia Water."

Next afternoon the three adventurers stepped off the coach at Windsor and joined the last conducted party filing through the Royal Apartments of Windsor Castle. Macdonnell found the whole excursion irrepressibly boring. He detested tradition and established order. The rooms of the apartments were stacked with priceless treasures.

"All useless," he grumbled. Ignoring the guide's droning patter, he gave his mind to other things. When they reached St. George's Hall he lit up a long cigar. Sharply, the guide looked round.

"No smoking . . ." He tailed off, staring closely at the offending tourist. Macdonnell was astonishingly like the Prince of Wales. He was the same age, and wore a similar light brown moustache and flowing beard.

"No smoking, if you please, sir," the guide amended cautiously. A conducted tour through his mother's home was the type of indulgence the Prince might find amusing.

Macdonnell stared at the guide insolently, took the cigar from his mouth and tossed it through the open window. Disregarding the gaping crowd he turned, with a Bidwell on each arm, and shepherded them down to the end of the 185-foot room. He began to talk quietly but enthusiastically.

"Reckon you had a good idea last night, Austin. About hitting the Bank of England," he said. "We need £25,000 each to make our journey worthwhile. The Old Lady is so loaded she would never miss the money. It is well for the lightning to strike where the balances are heavy."

"Agreed," said Austin happily.

George Bidwell's face hardened. He resented Macdonnell's scholarship, despised his recklessness.

"I understand the Bank of England is impregnable," he said shortly.

"As safe as the Bank of England!" Macdonnell dismissed the adage with a sweep of the hand. "A catchpenny phrase."

The tourist group was moving relentlessly forward. ". . . these portraits depict every ruling sovereign from James I to our beloved Queen," the guide intoned.

There was a knocking sound as Macdonnell tapped the paneling with his fist.

"Just as I expected," he said. "Hollow, completely hollow. So sounds the Bank of England. Still solid without, but riddled within by the dry rot of centuries."

George Bidwell turned impatiently away.

"Your assumptions are not founded on fact," he muttered as he rejoined the tourist party.

But Austin's brash suggestion, now seconded by Macdonnell, had begun to nag at George Bidwell's mind. It aggravated him during dinner at the Crown Hotel in the town and he ate in silence. Later, while Austin and Macdonnell scanned the public rooms for entertainment or a pretty face, George thought the problem over in a deep chair by the fire.

When the last resident had dropped his newspaper and shuffled off to bed George grew suddenly alert.

"Pull up your chairs, I want to speak to you quietly," he said.

Obediently, Austin and Macdonnell dragged their chairs into a semicircle round the fire. They lay back in their seats pulling at Turkish cigarettes.

"Well, Austin," George Bidwell said cheerfully, "I have decided you will become a customer of the Bank of England."

Austin choked on his cigarette. He sat up very straight.

"I beg your pardon?" he queried.

"We need to grow familiar with the inner workings of the bank. And you are the one to teach us," George told him calmly.

"Me?" Austin was horrified. "I have no credentials, no influential friends, no references."

"You may not require them," his brother said.

Austin considered the question. It was not breaking the law to become a customer of the Bank of England. It might prove amusing and instructive. He was sure he could act the part convincingly.

"Well, if you can fix it, George," Austin said finally. "I think it is an excellent idea."

"Good." George nodded understandingly at his brother. "Once you are established as a reliable customer, we must try to find a flaw in bank procedure. It will then be a simple matter to take advantage of it."

The three men dispersed in high spirits. They were enchanted by the notion of pitting their wits against the might of the Bank of England. The undertaking belonged to the romantic aspirations of another age.

2

AN
INNOCENT ACCESSORY

Every Wednesday for fifteen years Edward Hamilton Green, master tailor and army clothier, had carried the week's takings up the road and into the Western Branch of the Bank of England. He was a wealthy man. All well-dressed Englishmen came to Savile Row to have their suits made and Mr. Green had an extensive clientele.

On Wednesday, April 17th, a stranger scrutinized Green as he walked into the Western Branch. The same man was lingering on the pavement when the tailor re-emerged. He watched Green check through the stubs of his well-thumbed paying-in book, and followed him back down the road to 35 Savile Row.

Austin Bidwell had been watching the comings and goings at the Western Branch in Burlington Gardens for several days. His brother had decided that if he was to become a customer of the Bank of England the Western Branch might prove less formidable than the Head Office in Threadneedle Street. But even here it would be impossible to open an account without suitable references. Austin would have to find someone to vouch for him.

The Western Branch had been opened in 1855 as a convenience for gentlemen who found the journey from Mayfair to the City tedious, but highly respectable local tradesmen were also accepted as customers. It was amongst these solid citizens that Austin hoped to find a sponsor. He had narrowed his choice to three men;

an optician, an East India importer, and Mr. Green, the tailor.

Next morning Austin dressed with more than usual care and set out to investigate these unsuspecting candidates.

Entering the optician's shop first, Austin ordered the most expensive opera glasses on display. He asked to have them engraved. "To Lady Mary from HER FRIEND," and handed over a £100 note in payment. The optician took the note without the flicker of an eyelid, saying that the inscription would take several days. Austin left the shop realizing he had not yet found his man.

Next he visited the East India Importing House. He bought a costly silk shawl and agreed to take a camel-hair rug for twice as much again. When the importer tried to short-change him Austin knew he could not expect favors there.

It would have to be Mr. Green. Austin arrived on the doorstep of 35 Savile Row at 11:30 a.m. He was wearing a broad-brimmed stetson which made him look taller than his six feet. These hats were the accepted headgear of American tourists whose pockets were reputedly filled with rolls of notes. Austin lit up a cigar and swaggered into Mr. Green's shop.

In the warm, dark room he gradually discerned a semicircle of polished counters, red-shaded gaslamps, a crackling fire.

"Good morning, sir." An assistant stepped forward.

Austin strolled down the room and through the half-open curtains into the brilliantly lit stock-room. A lane of carpet stretched ahead, with bolts of cloth stacked to the ceiling on either side. Austin sauntered through, passing occasionally to examine a particular suiting. At last he stopped. He touched a light blue crombie lightly with his cane.

"Assistant," he called. "Please take a note. I require a frockcoat in this cloth, with silk sleeve facings and a velvet collar."

The assistant scurried up the room, pulling out his order book. Austin moved on again.

"Two pairs of trousers in this black and white cashmere," he rapped out. There was the sound of a door opening. The proprietor walked softly into the room. Mr. Green had heard the welcome overtones of a rich American accent. He had come to investigate.

"I require a fashionable city suit," Austin was saying. He tapped his cheek with the silver head of his cane, considering. Mr. Green stepped forward helpfully.

"Allow me to suggest this large-patterned worsted," he said. Austin turned slowly and stared down at the tailor. He saw a paunchy man of fifty-five, with a receding hairline, soft brown eyes, and accommodating smile.

Mr. Green introduced himself.

"Delighted, Mr. Green," Austin said. "You are just the man I was hoping to meet." Mr. Green was flattered.

The assistant had scribbled down orders for two frock-coats and five suits when Austin threw himself down into a chair.

"I reckon that's enough for today," he said with sudden disinterest.

"But, sir, you must have something to take away," Mr. Green protested. He reached out for the most expensive dressing-gown in stock.

"Our most beautiful robe," he said, stroking the rich blue brocade. "For twenty guineas."

"Thank you," said Austin.

While the tailor measured his new client, Austin complimented him on the superb range of fabrics in stock. He touched on his recent arrival in England and admitted a passion for English antiquities. He said he had come to London on business. He was acting for several large corporations with new inventions to expand in Europe. Mr. Green listened attentively. He warmed to his charming and influential client and discreetly asked for references so that he might open an account for him.

"Could you tell me your name, sir," he began tentatively.

"My name?" Austin queried sharply. He bit his lip in irritation. He had forgotten to arm himself with a suitable pseudonym.

"Warren," he said boldly. "My name is Warren."

"Would you fill in the customers' signature book, Mr. Warren, please. There is room for your references beneath."

Austin sat down and picked up the pen.

"Frederick Albert Warren," he wrote. "Golden Cross Hotel, London." He stared a moment at the two empty lines reserved for his references, then scraped back his chair and stood up. He smiled confidently down at Mr. Green.

"I'll pay cash for everything," he said. "There is no need to open an account. I'm not a resident. Be pleased to order me a cab."

Five minutes later Austin stepped out of 35 Savile Row and into a waiting cab. As the horse drew away from the curb, Austin sat back happily in the black hide seat. Discounting initial setbacks, the morning had turned out most successfully. He reviewed the scene at the tailor's shop, considering every detail of his own performance. Mr. Green had responded very favorably. With a little more expert handling the tailor would be well and truly hooked.

Austin climbed out of the cab at Charing Cross. He elbowed past the Americans crowding the entrance to the Golden Cross Hotel and approached the reception desk. There he registered a room in the name of Frederick Albert Warren in case Mr. Green inquired for him.

During the next fortnight Austin returned to Savile Row for two fittings, each time improving his acquaintance with Mr. Green. On the second occasion he surprised and delighted the tailor by ordering more clothes.

One day toward the end of April, Austin remarked casually to his brother, "I have found a sponsor."

George Bidwell was pleased but not surprised. Austin was an experienced confidence man. Men, and women particularly, were attracted by Austin's wit and invariable good humor. They were fascinated by his rare quality of detachment. A moustache blurred the outline of his thin lips, but acquaintances sometimes noticed that his eyes never smiled. Austin Bidwell was always watching for the main chance. It was this ruthlessness which had propelled him from an unpromising childhood to his present success.

He was the son of a South Brooklyn grocer. His father's frequent failures in business had bred in his sons a determination to succeed at any price. Austin's first job had been with a firm of sugar brokers. American business was expanding with intoxicating speed in the post-Civil War years, and the boom-town atmosphere in New York was infectious. Austin's duties round the sugar exchange brought him in contact with some of the sharpest operators on Wall Street and he took note of their methods.

When he moved to another brokerage house at the very good salary of $10 a week Austin met a well-connected young man named Ed Weeds. He achieved his first victory as a confidence man when he persuaded Ed to go into partnership with him. Weeds' wealthy father produced the initial capital and the new firm was incorporated E. Weeds & Co.

The next years were golden ones on Wall Street. With stocks booming and new ventures mushrooming overnight the young brokers were given many commissions and profits were high.

But Austin was quick to develop expensive tastes. The two young men frequented the theater, entertained the chorus with lavish dinners at Delmonico's and afterward gambled at the roulette tables. By daylight they were so exhausted that business suffered. Finally they

lost their entire capital. Weeds' father was persuaded
to pump in more funds, but the business crashed again.
Mr. Weeds senior dissolved the partnership and dispatched his son to Europe.

Austin Bidwell's personal bills continued to accumu-
late. He was haunted by memories of his father and
gambled furiously to regain financial stability. It was at
this juncture that he received a tempting offer from the
underworld. The approach was made one night after
Austin had lost at roulette and was drowning his sor-
rows at the bar. Would he be willing to dispose of a
cache of stolen bonds in Europe? Payment would be
handsome and his stockbroking experience ideally fitted
him for the job. It was undisguised crime, but a way out
of Austin's difficulties. He said "Yes."

He sailed for Europe, carried through the commission with a flourish and was back in New York a few
months later. With a cut of $13,000 in his pocket,
Austin decided to abandon legitimate work and had
achieved numerous successes as a con-man when he
reached London in 1872.

It was May 4th when Austin bowled up to Mr.
Green's shop for his third and final fitting. He was rid-
ing in a brougham. Tied to the carriage roof were two
portmanteaux and three hat-boxes, all empty. The spare
seats inside were stacked with four dressing bags, three
rugs, two silk umbrellas and two canes. This supple-
mentary luggage had been generously loaned by his two
friends.

Immediately Austin explained his mound of luggage
to Mr. Green.

"I am on the way to the station," he said. "I'm in-
vited to a few days' fishing in Ireland by Lord Clan-
carty. My driver is unroping a portmanteau. Kindly
pack my new clothes into it and dispatch it to 21 Enfield Road, Haggerstone."

"Of course, sir. At once, sir." Mr. Green sent an
assistant scurrying out to the cab. Austin watched coolly

as the man staggered back with an expensive leather traveling case appropriately monogrammed "F.A.W."

"Well, now, Mr. Green," he said, turning briskly to business. "I would like to settle my account." Austin pulled out of his wallet a brand-new £500 note.

Mr. Green swallowed.

"Your bill is only £150, sir," he said.

"Perhaps you will give me some change, in that case," Austin replied.

"If you will step into my office a moment," Mr. Green replied. "I will find it in the safe."

Mr. Green turned and led the way into his small office. He did not see the smile of pleasure which twisted the corners of Austin's mouth. The conversational lead-in had presented itself as he knew it would. Austin's quick mind slid through the questions and answers he required to reach his objective. He watched the strong-box door swing open, revealing ledgers and a cash-box, before dropping the loaded question.

"Oh, Mr. Green, how advantageous to possess a safe," he said. "I have more money than I care to carry with me to Ireland. Perhaps I could leave it with you."

Mr. Green did not look up—he was counting out the change.

"Why, of course, Mr. Warren," he said. "I will keep it in the cash-box and give you a receipt for the money."

Austin pulled out a roll of notes and began to count out his syndicate's reserves of cash.

"£500—600—900—1,000." The tailor looked up anxiously, he touched Austin's sleeve.

"It's too much, Mr. Warren," he protested. "I cannot take responsibility for so large a sum. You really should put it in your bank."

Austin stared blankly at Mr. Green. Like all ruthless men he was expert at turning on the pathos.

"I have no bank account, Mr. Green," he said sadly. "I am a visitor in your country."

The ruse worked perfectly.

"I'm sure we can attend to that, Mr. Warren. I will be delighted to introduce you to my bank. It is just at the end of the street."

The rest was routine. The two men stepped down the street and Austin was introduced to Mr. Fenwick, the assistant manager, who agreed to take care of the money. He deposited £1,000 in notes, £3 in mixed coin and a draft on the Continental Bank for £197— totalling £1,200. He signed the specimen signature book and gave his name: "Frederick Albert Warren, Golden Cross Hotel, London. Description 'Commission Agent.' " He thanked Mr. Fenwick warmly for his courtesy before asking the final question.

"I expect to complete a large business deal during the next few days," he told Mr. Fenwick. And then: "Should I ask Mr. Green to accompany me when I visit you again to deposit these considerable funds?"

"Not at all!" Mr. Fenwick explained. "You now have your own account with us. You can make remittances and withdrawals as you wish."

Five minutes later Austin Bidwell left the Western Branch with a check-book containing fifty checks.

That evening Frederick Albert Warren, Captain Bradshaw (George Bidwell) and Mr. Mapleson (Macdonnell) celebrated their success with dinner at the smart new Grosvenor Hotel in Victoria. The first assignment of the newly formed syndicate had passed off astonishingly well. It had taken only four weeks for Austin to persuade the Bank of England to accept a new customer without any of the usual references. A foreigner, with nothing more established for an address than one of the most cosmopolitan hotels in London. The dinner grew more hilarious as Austin recalled every detail of his con-manship until George Bidwell grew restive.

"This is all very excellent," he said, "but I should remind you that the Bank of England now possesses all our reserve funds." He looked accusingly across at

Austin. "It was reckless of you to promise further large deposits within days," he said tartly.

Austin stared blankly at his brother. It took only a few moments for the reproof to slide smoothly over his well-oiled back, and then he was smiling again.

"Well, boys," he said airily, "there is nothing for it but to make some money-raising forays into Europe." He smiled affectionately at his friends. "You should manage superbly," he said. "I will remain behind to soften up the bank."

3

THE
SPELLING MISTAKE

"Good morning, Mr. Warren, a very good morning to
you."

The doorman saluted smartly as Austin Bidwell
stepped through the imposing Portland-stone entrance
to the Western Branch. The man's white-gloved hand
inched forward invitingly.

"Good morning." Austin strode into the vast banking hall, forgetting to pass his usually generous tip to
the doorman.

They were anxious days. It was now three weeks
since his friends had left for Europe on a dangerous
assignment and Austin was beginning to fret for their
safety. At home funds were running embarrassingly
short. Austin stepped absent-mindedly across the marble
floor patterned with green and white diamonds. This
room was perhaps the most beautiful banking hall in
Europe. Despite its situation in the heart of London,
the place was filled with sunlight. There were long
windows on two sides. The 150-foot ceiling was divided
into eight sections, each containing a circular dome. A
curved Adam staircase led gracefully up to the Agent's
quarters. This fabulous room was originally the ban-
queting hall of Uxbridge House, town residence of Lord
Anglesey, and it was here that the one-legged Field
Marshal entertained his fellow heroes of Waterloo.

Austin reached the broad mahogany counter which
Philip Hardwicke, the early Victorian architect, had

installed for the bank. He smiled at the cashier through the gold-painted grille.

"Good morning, Coxgood," he said. "I have some dollars to pay in today."

He slid beneath the bars a thick roll of dollar bills. Austin was bent on establishing Mr. Warren, the new American depositor, as a rich and enterprising business-man. For a month he had been moving the only available £1,200 in and out of his account with a great show of activity. He had changed the cash into shares, into dollars, into drafts on other banks, and back again. The game was beginning to wear thin. Each day Austin watched sharply for a quickly concealed smirk amongst the cashiers.

When Austin arrived home that afternoon he noticed something unusual in the room. Macdonnell's boots were strewn across the floor. Austin leapt to the bed-room door and opened it. There was a sound of gentle snoring. The outline of his friend's body showed plainly under the coverlet—he had not waited to undress. George Bidwell and Macdonnell had arrived home ex-hausted after sweating it out in bank receiving rooms all over Europe. The climax of each interview was reached when managers scrutinized their credentials. These credentials composed a letter of credit from the Bank of South and North Wales and an introductory letter, or identification, from the manager of that bank. George Bidwell had procured the originals, under a false name, before he left London. But it was copies which the two friends were passing off in Berlin, Paris, Dresden, Bordeaux, Marseilles and Lyons. It only re-quired one sceptical manager to question the authenticity of the forged documents, by telegraphing their supposed place of origin, and instant exposure and arrest would follow.

"Never, never again," Macdonnell moaned when Austin roused him sixteen hours later.

"Yes, but where's the money?" Austin asked. At vast

expense of nervous energy the two men had procured
£4,000 to swell Mr. Warren's account. Austin tried
to hide his disappointment. It was really not sufficient
to cover their ambitious plans against the Bank of England.

But for once George Bidwell agreed with Macdonnell.

"We won't be going again," he said firmly. "It is too
hazardous to present forged documents in person." He
unscrewed a phial and swallowed down a stomach pill.
"It has ruined my digestion," he said.

An hour later Austin was watching his friends eat.
But his mind was busy turning over possible venues
for increasing their capital. All at once he relaxed.

"I have it!" he said. "I have the most wonderful
idea!"

"Oh, yes?" George Bidwell continued to shovel beef
and potatoes into his mouth. Austin was always proud
of his ideas, but they were not always inspired.

"South America, South America, my friends!" he
said. "There is no telegraph to South America. The
mail takes twenty days each way."

"Brilliant, Austin," said Macdonnell.

A week later the three men paid up their lodgings
and stored the surplus luggage. Mr. Warren informed
the cashiers at the Western Branch he was traveling to
St. Petersburg and southern Russia on business. He
would be away some months. The three men gave false
names when they purchased three round tickets for
South America at the Pacific Steam Navigation Company's offices in London.

It was June 16th, 1872, and a day of unruffled
tropical sunshine, when the steamship *Lusitania* carrying the Bidwells and Macdonnell ploughed through the
narrow gateway in the mountains which opened into the
Bay of Rio de Janeiro. Fertile green mountains closed
in the gap to the sea as the ship drove a furrow across
the mirrored surface of "Hidden Water," as the natives

called it. The gigantic bay was entirely surrounded by hills of every imaginable shape and color. Native fishing boats and small tropical islands dotted the surface of the eternally blue water. The three Americans, leaning on the deck-rail, felt they had strayed into a magic new world.

It was dusk when the *Lusitania* dropped anchor under the wall of the fort of Rio de Janeiro, and George Bidwell hurried to the writing-room. The syndicate had been popular among the passengers and George had been asked to compose an open letter of thanks on their behalf to the captain, which Macdonnell was to deliver before they went ashore. Macdonnell and Austin lingered on deck, watching the sun vanish in a burst of orange light behind the Organ mountains. A necklace of gaslamps threaded the curved harbor and stars of light climbed the velvet hills around.

This shipboard dream-world was shattered when the three men were rowed toward the town next morning. Perhaps every port is most attractive when viewed from a distance; this was certainly the case with Rio de Janeiro in 1872. The delicate odor, which had wafted across the water the night before, grew to a stench as the boat nosed the landing-stairs. It was apparent that sanitary requirements were low in Rio. In fact the town possessed no sewers at all. The noise was indescribable. Mornings are cool in Rio from May to August and the usually lethargic natives were bursting with high spirits. A law had been passed the previous year declaring that all future children of slave parents were free from the day they were born. Nevertheless a third of the population of Rio were still slaves and the port was thronged with gangs of Africans jabbering away in Congolese and other strange languages. They wore vividly colored pants and shirts as they humped stems of bananas, sacks of coffee, or baskets of oranges to the waiting boat.

The three Americans and their luggage were deposited on the stone quay, and the *Lusitania*'s cutter pulled back to the ship. They stood in a bewildered group, overwhelmed by the startlingly unfamiliar scene.

Macdonnell recovered first, and turned to a beggar. "Carriage," he said in fluent Portuguese. "We want a cab. You can have money if you find us a cab." He tried in Spanish, French and English, but it was useless. There were no cabs in Rio. Cab-drivers had abandoned the narrow congested streets in despair. Instead, a gang of coolies crowded round Macdonnell.

"Porter, sir, porter!" they jabbered. "I carry your bags."

The Negroes hoisted the heavy portmanteaux on to their heads and swung off down the cobbled street into the Rua Direita. The Americans divided, each booking into a separate hotel. Macdonnell was to act as "front man" in Rio. He spoke fluent Portuguese. In France he passed as a Frenchman; his Spanish and Italian were faultless. Macdonnell had been well educated by a succession of governesses and private tutors. He had grown up in the bosom of a wealthy New England family who lived in discreet taste on the outskirts of Boston. Their estate was separated from the outside world by an impenetrable evergreen hedge.

At seventeen, young George Macdonnell was tall and remarkably well proportioned. He had blue eyes and fair curling hair. His mother and young sisters doted on him, the servants spoiled him, his tutor admired his scholarship. Even his father, who had married late, was inordinately proud of his eldest son. But the boy was growing alarmingly headstrong and his father decided it was time he tested his resources against tougher opposition. He was entered for the Harvard Medical School with a view to his becoming a surgeon. The move proved a disaster. Freed from parental influence, Macdonnell could not wait to assert his independence. After four terms he threw up his studies and decamped to New York. On Wall Street he grew wildly excited by the bullish atmosphere of an expanding economy, and easily convinced himself, and his mother, that his natural gifts ideally suited him to be a stockbroker. His father was persuaded to loan $10,000, but Macdonnell possessed neither experience nor good judgment. He was endearingly, but fatally, prepared to indulge his own, and other people's, most reckless jests and enthusiasms. Reserves of cash dwindled fast. Then he ran up against Austin Bidwell. It proved the most disastrous encounter of his life. In no time at all he was completely fleeced and Austin was leading him into criminal practices. Austin had perceived that even without capital Macdonnell might be useful. He could provide a respectable and gentlemanly cover for Austin's ruthless aims and somewhat suspect charms.

Dressed as master and valet, the two young men covered the principal shops in New York, including Tiffany's, and lifted some choice merchandise, leaving dud checks in payment. Macdonnell ran into trouble when he tried to operate alone. He rode up to a cattle sale in Portland, Maine, and afterwards buttonholed the principal agent. They drank together until the agent grew incapable, when Macdonnell swiftly transferred to his own pockets the entire proceeds of the day's sale, totalling $10,000. The police cornered him two days later and at the tender age of twenty-two he was sentenced to two years in Sing Sing. His father refused to speak of him again.

In prison Macdonnell picked up the rudiments of forgery. He became fascinated by the artistry required to perfect an exact copy and directly he was released went in search of George Engels. Dubbed "Terror of Wall Street," this man was the leading exponent of forgery in America. Macdonnell became his pupil and proved himself an inspired duplicator.

It was only after Austin's urgent pleading that Macdonnell was included in the Bidwells' syndicate. George Bidwell was not impressed with Macdonnell. Despite his style and acknowledged expertise in duplicating,

George considered him highly strung and unreliable, and his Irish ancestry encouraged him to talk too much. Macdonnell sensed George Bidwell's reservations and was determined to show what he was made of in Rio.

Now in the ramshackle, mosquito-ridden hotel room he prepared his own letters of introduction to the leading banking house in South America, recommending they should honor his drafts for cash. He also made out a letter of credit drawn on the London and Westminster Bank in favor of "Mr. George Morris."

Next morning he threaded a path through a stream of bullock carts and pannier-laden mules on his way to present the documents to Maua and Company. He passed Negroes carrying giant bundles and women singing as they walked to the fountains with water pots on their heads. Wheelbarrows had once been imported into South America, but the practice was discontinued when Negroes insisted on carrying the barrows as well as the burdens on their heads. An inspired innovator had recently installed tramcars through the main thoroughfares to combat the lack of transport in the city. It was the sound of an approaching tram which drove the whole population suddenly berserk. Horses and mules broke into a gallop, dragging their carts behind them, pedestrians, dogs and children scattered to the safety of archways. Mac turned to see the monster tram burst round the corner of the street. It hurled itself down the narrow opening. Macdonnell leapt for the sidewalk, but there was none. Instead, he flattened himself against the vertical walls of a house. The tram shaved past him with a hideous clang and rattle, hurling a cloud of yellow dust over his clean white suit. Macdonnell wiped the grit from his eyes, but before he could pursue the prophetic implications of the incident his ears and senses were filled with the sound of rattle-boxes. The street was thronged again and a crowd of naked children jogged up and down to the monotonous sound of African music. Macdonnell shut his mind to evil portents, and

walked boldly into Maua and Company, where he pre-
sénted his credentials.

Next morning he was jubilant when he joined the
Bidwells under the striped awning of the café chosen
as their rendezvous.

"Astonishing! Fantastic!" he gloated, slapping a large
parcel down among the coffee-cups and glasses. He
threw himself into a cane armchair and helped himself
to Austin's rum.

"The bows! The courtesy! As they handed me
£8,000 of the firm's assets." Macdonnell's bray of
laughter startled surrounding customers.

" 'Allow us to pack it in a parcel, señor,' they said!"

George Bidwell's eyes narrowed. "Keep your voice
down," he snapped. He lifted with both hands the
heavy parcel of Brazilian banknotes, for everything
above fourpence was paper money in Brazil, and slipped
it carefully into a leather case at his feet.

"Austin, you have already made inquiries at the exchange," he said quietly. "Go there immediately and
change these notes to sovereigns. With them buy Portuguese bonds."

"O.K." Austin gestured to the waiter for the bill.
"Gee, that was a pretty excellent piece of business," he
told his friend as he searched in his pocket for change.
He looked up, regarding his brother steadily. "Don't
you agree, George?" he asked.

"Yes, yes, excellent," George conceded. "Just the
type of capital we require right now."

They had paid the bill and were moving into the
street when Macdonnell informed them blithely, "I have
requested twice as much in a week's time."

Austin stared at his friend.

"Superb, Mac, superb," he said.

Macdonnell shrugged. "We must harvest where the
plums are ripest," he said, kicking out at a half-eaten
melon in the street. It exploded in a mess of pink flesh
and pips.

A week later the Bidwells watched Macdonnell swing
in through the portals of Maua and Company to collect
£16,000. George Bidwell glanced at his watch. He
detested this type of scatterbrained exploit, entailing
minimum planning and maximum risk. It was 11 a.m.
The transactions at the bank should take barely five
minutes—providing nothing went wrong. George Bidwell shut out the hideous thought and settled down to
wait.

Immediately Macdonnell spoke to the cashier at the
counter he sensed something uncomfortable. He remembered the man as a bored but courteous official.
Now he was wary.

"Mr. George Morris?" he said. "The manager is engaged for the present. Will you step into the waiting-
room?"

Alone, in an airless room twelve feet by ten, Macdonnell began to simmer with rage. He had never been
able to wait quietly. Inaction drove him insane. He
leafed through the supplied literature, lit up a cigar
and began to pace the room. A Macdonnell kept waiting by the manager of a bank—a Brazilian bank. It was
disgusting. That Macdonnell's aim was to lift a fortune
from the firm was quite beside the point.

Macdonnell picked up his hat and swept through
the door immediately the bank servant came to show
him to the manager's office. He stepped into the room.

"Good morning, gentlemen," he said, his blue eyes
blazing with fury.

The manager did not stand up and shake hands. He
stared suspiciously across at Macdonnell and picked up
some papers from his desk. Macdonnell looked round
for a chair. The only one available was occupied by a
well-greased Brazilian, wearing a black frock-coat and
white trousers. The man showed no inclination to move.

"I am the stockbroker of Maua and Company," he
informed Macdonnell severely. The atmosphere in the
hot room was less than cordial.

"Is your name Mr. George Morris?" the manager queried, flicking over the pages of Macdonnell's credentials.

"It certainly is," Macdonnell snapped.

"And are these your credentials?" He tapped the papers in his hand.

"They are."

The manager's lips tightened. "There is an error of spelling in this letter of credit," he said.

Macdonnell flushed. "Is that so?" he asked. His concern was genuine. The implications of the error were instantly and hideously apparent.

"Is it not strange that clerks of the London and Westminster Bank cannot spell the word 'endorse'?" the manager demanded.

The sweat was breaking out along Macdonnell's backbone.

"It is absolutely scandalous," he agreed. "May I see the document?"

He accepted the letter, studying it with a coolness he did not feel.

"It is a disgraceful oversight," he said. "I would not consider allowing you to cash this letter of credit," Macdonnell folded the letter into his wallet.

"Thank you, gentlemen," he said. "I have letters of credit to other banking houses in your city. They will no doubt oblige with the capital I currently require."

As he turned away there came the harsh scrape of chairs on polished wood.

"I would like to see those letters of credit," the manager demanded.

Macdonnell gulped. The broker was strolling casually between himself and the door. He turned slowly back to the manager.

"I am astonished by my treatment at Maua and Company," he said. His lips moved in a small prayer of thanks to George Bidwell who had provided for this type of emergency by insisting Macdonnell should carry forged letters of introduction and credit to other firms besides Maua and Company. Macdonnell slipped these letters from his pocket and dropped them lightly on the desk. The manager read them through grudgingly. His suspicions were temporarily mollified and Macdonnell was allowed to leave the premises unmolested.

The Bidwells' relief to see Macdonnell walk out into the sunlit street was tempered by his empty hands and flushed and furious face. They followed him warily down side-streets to an unobtrusive café. Emergency plans raced through their heads. Hearing Macdonnell's story intensified their anxiety. They hustled him to the docks and smuggled him on to the *Ebro*, leaving for Europe in a couple of hours.

Next morning they collected all the luggage and boarded the *Chimborazo* bound for Montevideo.

Macdonnell's superb presence of mind and the Bidwells' prompt action had averted any serious consequences resulting from the spelling mistake. But the zest had gone from their piratical excursion to the Spanish Main. The brothers had lost their confidence as well as their interpreter. At Montevideo they picked up a consolation prize for Macdonnell. It was a handsome gold-knobbed cane with a diamond-eyed snake curled round the shaft. They caught the next boat to Europe.

It was August when the ebullient trio climbed out of the boat-train at Victoria Station. They were bronzed and bouncing, £12,000 richer from their European and South American forays, and spoiling for richer gains.

An avalanche of plans was pouring through George Bidwell's mind. He intended to keep a firm hold on the Bank of England project. Stupid errors would be eliminated. Brains, inventiveness and care were required when huge fortunes were going to be made.

4

THE
LOOPHOLE

In the narrow cobbled alley leading off Finsbury Circus, George Bidwell turned into a doorway which said "Licensed to Sell Spirits and Caterer." Bidwell had scoured the City coffee houses street by street before he discovered this ideal rendezvous, central but inconspicuous. Inside, the café was dingy but clean. There were half a dozen marble-topped tables, some rickety chairs, and faded prints of country scenes pasted to the dark brown walls. A red-handed, chunky young man in shirt-sleeves behind the counter nodded non-committally at Bidwell. The young man's reserve had impressed him on his first visit when George had discovered that he was a countryman, new to the neighborhood, and that the café was his first independent venture. Bidwell had offered him a few shillings' rent for the use of a small back room, and the man accepted. The room had become George Bidwell's "office." It was the only place where he was prepared to meet or contact Macdonnell and Austin during daylight hours.

When George Bidwell pushed open his office door he was surprised to find his friends already in occupation.

"Good morning," he said briskly.

There was a half-empty bottle of red wine and three glasses on the scrubbed wooden table. Macdonnell leaned over and poured George a glass, while Austin shifted some tins of biscuits from a chair, and dragged it forward. Nobody spoke. George Bidwell sat down and swallowed a drink. He looked into his brother's face. The silence was a happy change from the incessant banter he usually endured from the others, but he sensed their anxiety.

"What's the trouble?" he asked.

Austin looked grave. "Well, George," he said, "we were on our way down the Strand this morning when we spotted someone we all know."

"Who was that?"

"Big Bill Pinkerton."

George Bidwell tensed like a cat. Pinkerton was a detested name in American criminal circles. His agency was the one incorruptible force working for law and order over the entire American continent. George questioned his brother closely. Was he certain it was Pinkerton, was he alone, had he noticed them, or followed?

In fact Pinkerton had recognized both Austin Bidwell and Macdonnell. He had arrived in London on the trail of some Baltimore bank robbers, but had pointed out the friends to Detective Inspector Shore of Scotland Yard and outlined forceably to him the type of activities he might expect from them. As a result, Scotland Yard circulated all the London banks warning them that a coup might be contemplated. It was a warning that never penetrated the cast-iron confidence of the Bank of England.

George Bidwell listened to all his brother could tell him about the Pinkerton encounter.

"There is nothing he can pin on us," he decided confidently, "but I recommend you both to change your address and adopt other aliases."

The three men had moved from seclusion in the suburbs to the heart of fashionable London. But George refused to occupy the same house as his brother in Langham Street. Above everything, he wished to remain unobtrusive and anonymous, and the family likeness between himself and Austin might be memorable. He took rooms at Nelson's Hotel in Portland Place.

George Bidwell picked up his Gladstone bag, ferreted through it, and drew out a scroll tied with red ribbon. He handed it to Austin. Inside was a painting on vellum of a coat of arms. Macdonnell blushed for his friends. The Bidwells professed to be descendants of the old Saxon Biddulphs and George had pressed Messrs. Wyon of Regent Street to find the Bidwell crest. Finally, an assistant named Russell had mocked up a fine conglomeration of heraldic signs.

"Three crossed martlets, four fishes and two ships." Austin bent over the picture, his eyes gleaming with family pride.

"Ding, dong, bell! My ancestors are all in hell!" Macdonnell stretched out his arms and yawned luxuriously. The Bidwells folded the scroll away and got down to business.

During the last two weeks the three men had been making exhaustive inquiries in the City. They were now familiar with British business methods, but they were no further ahead with a plan for taking advantage of them.

George produced a packet of visiting cards. Across the center of each was printed, "Frederick Albert Warren" in shaped Victorian capitals.

"It is time Mr. Warren returned from southern Russia," he said, "and paid his compliments to the leading official of the Western Branch."

On September 3rd the three-faced clock of All Souls' Langham Place was striking 10 a.m. when Austin and Macdonnell emerged into the early autumn sunshine. They looked up at the racing clouds and set off down Regent Street to the Bank.

Austin listened perfunctorily to Macdonnell's reassuring chatter. He had dressed with particular care, but still fidgeted with his cravat. One of the diamond rings on his long fingers glinted in the sunlight. Austin sucked in his breath.

"Are my rings too pretentious?" he asked abruptly, struggling to free one from his knuckle.

"No, no, they're just fine," Macdonnell quieted him.

Austin was dithering with nervous excitement. He was approaching the crucial first interview with the senior official of the Western Branch. The outcome of the encounter could make or mar their future plans. Austin possessed a high opinion of his gifts as a confidence man, but some personalities were undeniably less susceptible than others. Fervently he hoped the manager had been endowed with a reasonably pliable nature.

The two men reached the right-hand turn to Old Burlington Street. Macdonnell pressed his friend's arm.

"So long, pal," he said, and turned into a tobacconist's. "Mr. Warren" strode on alone to his appointment.

Austin was received by a bank messenger wearing a cut-away, salmon-pink tailcoat and a crimson waistcoat with silver buttons. The resplendent figure held out a silver salver for Mr. Warren's visiting card, crossed the passage to the agent's room, and formally introduced his visitor. Austin immediately recognized the man who stepped forward to greet him. It was Mr. Fenwick, the sub-agent. They shook hands, and Fenwick drew Mr. Warren forward to meet his new superior, the agent of the Western Branch.

Across a large, cluttered desk, Austin stared into the humorous eyes of Colonel Peregrine Madgwick Francis. The Colonel rose to his feet and it was evident why he had recently achieved this plum position at the Bank of England's No. 1 social branch. He was a man of obviously cultured background, who was also immediately likeable. Expansive, witty and sympathetic, it was unnecessary for him to display great energy or pay attention to detail. He possessed an experienced and reliable staff.

Austin was filled with new buoyancy as he sat down opposite the Colonel. He was certain they would get on remarkably happily. Refusing a cigar, he laid on the desk £8,000 of Portuguese bonds which he asked the Colonel to take care of. He then launched confidently into an imaginary tale of his expanding business interests. First and foremost he was hoping to introduce Pullman's Palace Sleeping Cars into Europe. These sleeping cars had revolutionized rail travel in America but were so far unknown on this side of the Atlantic. There were sundry other inventions which he hoped to develop, including a steam-brake.

The Colonel had been listening with polite attention, but now his eyes lit with interest.

"I would be fascinated to hear further details of your steam-brake," he said, leaning forward so as not to miss a word.

Impassively Austin stared at Colonel Francis. He sensed danger, although he did not know the Colonel had spent his youth as an engineer in the Indian Army and steam-brakes were a subject he could understand.

Austin shook his head. "I'm sorry, Colonel," he said, "I'm afraid I cannot reveal details of the steam-brake. It's highly confidential."

His conversation leapt deftly back to the safer ground of Pullman cars. It appeared that Mr. Warren was determined to have them running from Paris to Vienna in time for the Vienna Exhibition in May of the following year. He would be searching for contracts on the Continent and manufacturing facilities in England. Each of the cars cost £4,000 and he would need to finance the building contractors with large sums.

"It might even be necessary to request credit facilities from time to time," he said cautiously.

"We will be glad to accommodate you in every way we can, Mr. Warren," the Colonel assured him.

That was all Austin wished to know. "Well, Colonel, I have business to attend to," he said.

Austin got up, leaned across the desk and grasped the Colonel warmly by the hand. "Good afternoon," he said and disappeared briskly from the room.

The Colonel took a few more drags at his cigar. He was sorry to hear no more details of the steam-brake.

His mind went back through the years, recapturing a picture of the heat and dust of road-building in India, the rough ride back to barracks, a game of polo in the cool evening. He was still reminiscing as he closed Mr. Warren's file.

The three Americans paid up their lodgings and once again dispersed to the Continent. Checks and drafts began to pour into Mr. Warren's account from a dozen different banks in Paris, Vienna, Frankfurt, Amsterdam, Hamburg and Rotterdam. Mr. Warren would seem to be achieving results with his sleeping-car enterprise.

But the Americans felt only frustration. During September and October they searched in vain for a flaw in the financial structure of Europe. Austin alone reckoned he covered over 10,000 miles on the Continent negotiating bankers' drafts and buying bonds and bills of exchange. Owing to restricted capital all their assets had to be sold every few days, and frequently at a loss. Broker's fees added to the mounting costs of train fares and hotel accommodation.

The habitual hazards of foreign travel with changing currencies, language, and customs were intensified by a mounting feeling of urgency as each new road ended in a false trail. George was driven to exasperation by the cautious attitude of the Dutch in Amsterdam and Rotterdam. Austin found intolerable the efficiency of German businessmen in Frankfurt and Hamburg and was driven to enjoy a few days' relaxation at Baden Baden. In Paris Macdonnell could find no line to exploit in French dealings on the Bourse.

It was on a note of desperation that George and Macdonnell arrived in Vienna and booked into the Rheinischer Kaiser Hotel, preparatory to making inquiries into Austrian monetary practice. Here a further inconvenience overtook them. Macdonnell fell ill with malaria. George immediately telegraphed his brother, and Austin replied reassuringly to his sick friend:

My dear M—I am more sorry than I can tell to hear you are suffering so much. G. has just telegraphed that you shall not be governed by the thought that we wish you to go on at once. Far from it; the first consideration is your health and if you require rest for ten days more for heaven's sake take it. I remain yours truly "A."

George Bidwell's daily visits to the Vienna Bourse were sandwiched between hours of sick-bed duty. George approached his role of male nurse with an intensity Macdonnell found alarming. Electrical treatment was then the panacea for all ailments. George therefore bought a galvanic battery and subjected his feverish patient to a series of electric shocks. As soon as he could walk Macdonnell hobbled on to a train with the aid of of two sticks. He was retreating to London to consult his personal physician.

By some extraordinary good fortune Macdonnell stopped in Rotterdam to convert his foreign currency. But it was not until he visited his London bank two days later that he realized he had inadvertently stumbled on the opening they had been searching for so long. He walked straight to the nearest post office and telegraphed George and Austin:

HAVE MADE A GREAT DISCOVERY. COME IMMEDIATELY. MAC.

Twenty-four hours later the Bidwells were back in town. They surprised Macdonnell devouring fried sole and strawberries in his room at the Alexandra Hotel, Hyde Park Corner. He greeted them delightedly and rang for two more covers for breakfast.

Tilting his chair back, he grinned triumphantly up at his accomplices.

"Did you happen to know that in London bills of exchange are paid on sight?" Macdonnell began to explain.

In Rotterdam he had converted his foreign currency into a bill of exchange on Baring Bros., the impeccable City merchant bankers. Bills of exchange have been the principal instruments for transferring money from one country to another for 3,000 years. Originally they were notes given to foreign merchants by long-distance traders ordering large consignments of goods. The notes promised payment when the goods were delivered. They became known as bills of exchange. Over the years the bills themselves became legal tender. They were always dated for payment by the issuing house three or more months ahead.

"Directly I arrived in London I drove to the London and Westminster bank and paid in the bill of exchange," Macdonnell continued. "I was astonished to be paid in cash immediately."

"It's unbelievable," Austin said.

George Bidwell picked up his cane and gloves; he was halfway to the door.

"What's wrong?" Austin queried sharply.

"I'm going to try and cash a bill of exchange," George Bidwell growled.

One hour later he was back and ordering champagne for his breakfast. He had visited the bank and come out with a walletful of notes. Macdonnell had been perfectly correct. In England it was standard practice to pay out immediately on bills of exchange. George Bidwell was jubilant. In America such bills were always sent back to the issuing house for verification and initialing before being honored. Yet here in London there was no such precautionary routine. Between the date of issue of a bill of exchange and its maturing three months later no check was made of its authenticity by the bank. The whole procedure was based on the satisfactory reputation of the customer who presented the bill for discount.

It meant that if the Americans could manufacture their own bills of exchange skillfully enough for them to be acceptable to the Bank of England these bills could be deposited in Mr. Warren's account. Cash would be paid out on the bills immediately, and there would be a clear three months before the bank returned the bills to their supposed issuing house and discovered they were forgeries. This would leave ample time for Mr. Warren and his associates to vanish.

At last they had discovered the flaw in British monetary practice which they had begun to fear did not exist. They were as delighted and astonished as if they had been handed the keys of the Bank of England vaults.

Only one thought troubled George Bidwell.

"Will the Bank of England accepts bills of exchange for discount from Frederick Albert Warren?" he asked anxiously.

"I will find out first thing in the morning," Austin assured him.

5

NELLIE

A cab took George Bidwell from the Alexandra Hotel up through the Park to Ford's Hotel, Manchester Square. At the desk he asked for Mr. Bidwell's suite and was led upstairs to a high-ceilinged room with a pair of French windows opening to a small balcony above the square. The furniture was institutional but attempts had been made to personalize the room. A new tartan traveling rug draped the olive-green settee. French novels lay scattered over the oak table. Above the fireplace polished shells were reflected in the mirrored gilt overmantel. Bidwell's red carpet-slippers had been placed discreetly by the unlit fire.

George strode into the bedroom. The curtains were drawn. There was a girl asleep in the bed. Bidwell could not decide if she was naked, for the white sheet reached up to her short, straight nose. Her cool, unlined forehead was framed by a crop of boyish curls. The girl stirred, opening her eyes. She reached up a soft hand and touched Bidwell on the sleeve.

"Pardon, chéri," she whispered huskily. "I was so tired."

The girl smelled warm and sweet. In a rough gesture Bidwell stripped back the sheet, muttering coarse endearments.

It was on a hot day in August that George Bidwell had first met Nellie Vernon. She had a child on her arm when she slipped into a vacant seat beside him on a bus traveling south from Euston Station. The child

47

took an instant liking to Bidwell. Despite Nellie's re-proofs, he clambered on to the stranger's knee and pressed his small face against his chest. George Bidwell had a wife and small son in America, and the child made him homesick. When the bus reached Charing Cross he hoisted the boy on to his shoulder and carried him down to watch the boats on the river. Serenely, the girl accompanied them. She was small and well dressed in a mauve silk jacket and skirt of a darker shade, looped neatly over a bustle at the back. She was extremely pretty and her voice had a lilting French accent which made a disquieting impression on George Bidwell.

"Is he your child?" he asked her curiously.

"Non, non, monsieur. A little friend, the son of my landlady."

She told him she was Belgian and eighteen years old. They stopped to buy a bun for the boy; he ate half. When Nellie leaned against the enbankment to throw the rest to the gulls her breasts brushed Bidwell's hand. Sharply he drew his hands away. A passion both violent and protective flooded through him.

"I must meet you alone," he breathed. His tone star-tled Nellie. She did not look at him or answer, but stared vacantly across the river. The innocence of the outing had been broken, Nellie laughed no longer, George grew broodingly obstinate, the child began to whine.

It took George Bidwell one month to gain his ob-jective. He loaded Nellie with presents, took her to the opera and out to dine, and seduced her in Room 64 of the Victoria Hotel, St. Leonards. The girl was caught up in the fierceness of his passion and willingly accom-panied him to the Grand Hôtel de Paris in Trouville. Here Bidwell left her alone all day—he had business commitments. Nellie was lonely and bored. She wan-dered across the sandy beach wearing a narrow-brimmed sailor's hat and pink silk dress. She wore gloves and carried a pale gray parasol. She picked up shells at the water's edge, but perspiration was dribbling down her back. She retreated indoors. The hotel was stuffy and jammed with potted plants. Upstairs she unlaced her brown kid shoes and stepped out of her dress. She skipped across the room in a white lawn chemise with drawers reaching to the knee, unclipped Bidwell's case and examined his correspondence. She found letters from his wife and bills and drafts made out in a dozen false names.

Nellie was a practical girl. She did not indulge in accusations and hysteria, but she told George Bidwell that evening that she felt ill and wished to go home.

But her restricted circumstances in the household in Duke's Road, Euston Square, played on Nellie's nerves. She grew short-tempered and irritable, and lived for the passionate letters which arrived from Paris, Hamburg and Vienna. After two months she packed her clothes and rejoined Bidwell in Holland. She agreed to live with him, called herself Mrs. Bidwell, was favored with presents and affection, but she asked no questions and received no explanations. By keeping closed the communicating door between his mistress and his other activities Bidwell could justify flouting one of the basic rules in criminal behavior—no womanizing.

But something infinitely more serious now threatened to wreck the Americans' plans. When Austin made inquiries at the Western Branch he discovered that bills of exchange were not acceptable for discount there. Bills of exchange were only discounted at headquarters, as a favor, to customers known personally to one of the twenty-four directors. It was a setback which would have floored men less determined than the Bidwells. They inquired on the Continent which bills were most readily acceptable at the Bank of England, and purchased two of them. On November 29th Austin Bidwell walked into the Western Branch. After an exchange of affabilities with Colonel Francis he presented the bills for discount.

Colonel Francis looked at Mr. Warren in surprise.

"But we never accept bills of exchange for discount at the Western Branch," he said.

Austin stiffened in his chair. He looked genuinely astonished.

"But you agreed to give me certain discount facilities," he said in a shocked tone. "And these bills are first-class paper."

Anxiously he stood up from his seat opposite the Colonel and moved round the desk with the bills in his hand.

"You will see the acceptors are marked as Suse and Sibeth," he said earnestly.

The Colonel took the bills and stared reflectively at them. They were each made out for £500, payable on February 3rd, 1873. He shifted in his chair, uncomfortably aware of Austin's dominating presence.

"I understand from reliable sources on the Continent that the Bank of England would be pleased to accept bills of exchange on Suse and Sibeth," Austin said.

Colonel Francis admired his client's eagerness and enterprise. Mr. Fenwick had assured him that this new American customer was "very clear, accurate and particular" in business matters.

"Very well," he said amicably. "I will make inquiries at the Bank of England this afternoon. Perhaps they will make an exception in this case."

Austin's eyes widened. A feeling of something like affection for Colonel Francis swept through him. He strode back to his chair and picked up his umbrella and hat.

"Good afternoon, Colonel," he said gently.

He never said "Thank you" for favors received, it only encouraged second thoughts.

That afternoon Colonel Francis took the bills down

to the Bank of England and was given permission to discount them.

Taken out of context, such free-handed generosity by the Bank of England appears astonishingly unbusinesslike. In effect it was a favor granted to Colonel Francis in respect of the two bills he presented, and not expected to be taken as authority for numerous bills of a similar kind to be discounted for a new customer. The gesture was willfully misconstrued by Austin Bidwell and from that day Mr. Warren, the unique customer without references or permanent address, was numbered among the very influential few who discounted bills of exchange at the Bank of England.

Austin Bidwell was tremendously excited when he marched into the small back room of the coffee house near Finsbury Circus. He had achieved the impossible once again.

"They have accepted the bills for discount. We have them beaten," he told his brother. George Bidwell was sitting at the table surrounded by a sea of paperwork. His granite eyes gleamed with delight.

"Very good," he said. "We can now continue with our prearranged plan."

"I have a better idea," Austin said. "The whole matter can be ended in one swift decisive stroke. We can be back in New York for Christmas."

"Well?"

"I have only to present £50,000 in forged bills at the Western Branch and the whole amount will be discounted to me immediately," he said.

George Bidwell considered the tempting suggestion for a moment. They had already spent thousands of pounds in preparation; they were all exhausted by their expeditions to the Continent; it would be an immense relief to end the project swiftly.

"You would be overloaded leaving the bank with fifty bags containing a thousand sovereigns," George said sourly.

"I'd take it in banknotes."

"Each with an identification number? You must be insane. I would not consider such a scatterbrained idea," he said severely.

Austin swallowed his frustration. He watched his brother cross to the far corner of the room. George bent down, unlocked the catches of a battered cabin trunk, and swung back the lid.

Austin stared curiously at the contents.

"What in heaven's name is all that rubbish?" he asked.

Over the last months George Bidwell had developed the most compulsive habit. Wherever he went on the Continent he methodically visited the stationers' shops, laying in an enormous stock of various papers, colored inks, sealing wax, pens, nibs, rubber stamps and other supplies which might prove useful in forging documents. Recently he had begun to pick up blank bill of exchange forms, which were obtainable at any large stationer's.

"I have blank bill of exchange forms printed in French, German, Italian, Russian, Turkish and Arabic," he said proudly.

Now that the time had come to manufacture the forged documents this paraphernalia would be wonderfully useful.

"Where on earth has Macdonnell got to?" George Bidwell growled.

Macdonnell had been absent eight days on an errand which should have taken twenty-four hours. Much that appears on a bill of exchange is virtually impossible to reproduce by hand and Macdonnell had been dispatched to Paris to contact skilled artisans to produce the printing blocks he needed, rather than risk the least suspicion by employing men in London.

Two days later the Bidwells found Macdonnell back in residence when they reached the "office." He was sitting in George's chair with his feet up on the desk.

Casually, Macdonnell looked over his newspaper.

"Good morning," he said.

George Bidwell felt his temper rising.

"Well?" he said sharply. "Did you find some reliable engravers in Paris?"

Macdonnell turned the paper to the foreign news page.

"There are no wood engravers in Paris," he said. His voice sounded elaborately bored. George Bidwell clenched his teeth.

"That is complete and utter nonsense." he snapped.

Austin regarded Macdonnell anxiously. In a city of one and a half million people there must be a hundred block-makers. Surely his friend had not decided to back out of the enterprise? His skill in forgery was indispensable now.

Macdonnell was in an ugly mood. During the ten wasted days in his beloved Paris he had suffered a crisis of disenchantment with the Bidwells and the Bank of England project. Initially he had been fascinated by the intellectual problem of finding a crack in the seemingly impregnable façade of the Bank of England. Now he had discovered it, the challenge was over, and Macdonnell's polished mind shied away from the tedious details required to bring the scheme to fruition. He felt bored, and faintly revolted, by the Bidwells' frenetic eagerness. And so George Bidwell was forced to discard his original intention of remaining in the background to organize the coup. If block-makers had to be found in London the task of dealing with them would need patience and discretion. He considered he was the best man for the job.

Out of a City directory he tore the pages appertaining to the engravers and lithographers, and underlined those firms with premises in and around Paternoster Row.

Early the next day George Bidwell drove to the City. It was a filthy late November morning. Rain poured vertically down, drenching everything. As the cab jolted to a standstill he stepped gingerly on to the pavement. It was slippery with mud and slime flung up by passing carriages and carts. Hoisting his umbrella, he paid off the driver and stared curiously down "The Row," center of the London book-publishing trade at a time when the average leather-bound book cost three shillings. Between the tall buildings housing the firms of Longmans, Blackwoods and Simpkin Marshall there were sandwiched doorways and unpretentious shop windows, hiding dingy workshops where all the small requirements of the printing trade were manufactured.

George Bidwell felt water oozing over the tops of his shoes. He glanced down. His feet had sunk completely into mud, which reached to his trousers. With a shrug, he sloshed down the street to interview the first name on his list. He turned into the premises of Carter and Dalton, 21 Paternoster Row.

The man who moved forward from the back shop wore a flannel shirt with rolled-up sleeves and a leather apron over his trousers. He was a great tree of a man with soft brown eyes and a loose mouth. He did not speak.

"Guten morgen," George said. "I have work to be done in block-making. You show me some specimens of the work you do, please."

He hoped that his imitation of a German accent passed muster. The man's blank face gave him no clue.

"Specimens," George repeated loudly. "I would like to see specimens of your work."

The man lifted his right hand to a level with his face. Between his fingers was a dog-eared card, rectangular and bordered with ornate scrolls. George read the message printed on it. "I am James Dalton, I am totally deaf." George smiled delightedly at Mr. Dalton. Here was a piece of good luck: a man requiring no difficult answers. Carefully, Bidwell wrote down his instructions on a sheet of paper and printed beneath them: "Read back." A shudder swept the large man's body, his mouth opened so wide Bidwell could see the palpitating tonsils. Obscene words welled up from Dalton's throat. With a convulsive effort he achieved the first word. Relentlessly, George Bidwell waited until the whole message had been repeated to him.

George Bidwell visited forty firms within the next three days. The employees were not all so obviously suitable as Mr. Dalton, but eventually Bidwell picked out a team of five: James Dalton and William Cheshire, engravers; George Challoner of Nelsons, the printers; James Straker, a printer and lithographer; and William Mitchell, die-sinker and stamp-cutter. Between them these five men would manufacture dozens of small pieces, reproductions of genuine bills which would fit together to make forged bills of exchange.

Back in Langham Street, Austin was trying to persuade Macdonnell to settle to some work. It was an uphill job. Macdonnell complained he was tired, sick, hungry, bored. His surroundings were too restricted, the light inadequate, the table unsteady. Very well, they would move, Austin decided.

On December 1st Austin and Macdonnell moved into a large double room at the Grosvenor Hotel, Victoria. They were entered on the accommodation list as Captain Bradshaw and Mr. Mapleson. The hotel had recently been built beside the principal Continental departure station. It was fashionable and exclusive. The service was good and the waiters even wore white gloves to serve meals. But the food was horrible. Uncompromising roast beef and potatoes, turnips or cabbage, followed by apple tart, tasted flat to epicures like Austin and Macdonnell. The bedroom would do excellently as a workroom, but they decided to dine elsewhere.

Half-heartedly, Macdonnell assembled his tools: a large selection of nibs and inks with which to copy handwriting, tracing papers, rulers, a magnifying glass and a small printing machine. George Bidwell's battered trunkful of stationery was brought in.

Austin boarded the night train to the Continent and returned with a handful of top-quality bills of exchange. Examining them, Macdonnell was suddenly interested. Here was a challenge to his pride. To forge acceptances of the greatest firms in London, or the world. He went to the desk and sat down.

Over the next weeks Macdonnell hardly moved from the bedroom. He subsisted on sandwiches and coffee brought up by a waiter, and if Austin persuaded him out to dine he excused himself after two courses and hurried back to Grosvenor and his duplicating. Notes were dispatched to George Bidwell with tracings of scrolls and lettering, dates and numbers and company seals, with instructions that each should be copied and the blocks mounted in a holder with a handle. Now that Macdonnell's interest was roused, he was transformed from a wastrel to a genius. His patience with minute detail, fitting together, copying and printing, was inexhaustible.

It was about three o'clock one afternoon, and already dusk, when Austin unlocked the bedroom door. Macdonnell was crouched over the desk, his head resting on his arms. He woke immediately.

"Here, Austin, say which is false and which is true." He brandished a fistful of bills of exchange in each hand.

Austin moved over and examined the bills in the pool of light. It was impossible to distinguish the forged bills, except that the dates of acceptance and amounts of payment were missing.

Austin's heart slumped as he studied them. However perfect they appeared, he was faced with the prospect of presenting a succession of forged bills at the Western Branch. All bills of exchange were examined by a skilled committee of the Bank of England before they were lodged in the customer's file. He could not distinguish the forgeries, but would they? One slip, one false word or hesitation on his part, and the whole scheme would come crashing about his ears. He would have no possible defense if he were caught passing forged bills across the counter or walking out of the bank carrying thousands of pounds of the Bank of England's own money.

6

THE
TAKE-AWAY MAN

On the morning of December 2nd George Bidwell struggled up Poultry, his long, belted ulster buttoned to his chin. The Mansion House looked forlorn in the enveloping drizzle. George trudged the length of the rusticated lower story and turned up the approach stairway. He wondered what strange arguments had persuaded City aldermen to build this romantic, Palladian-type villa at so riotous a road junction as residence for the Lord Mayor.

George reached the fourth step and halted. He had a clear view over the bustling traffic to doorway No. 79 at the beginning of Lombard Street. It was the headquarters of the Continental Bank. Watching the stream of businessmen moving in and out of the bank, George thought over details of his cunning new plan to absolve Austin from removing in person the funds they hoped to receive from the forgeries.

He nearly missed his brother as he left the bank. Even Austin's walk was different and the square-cut suit, chunky boots and stetson hat seemed to belong to a bluffer personality. George saw him lift a badly furled umbrella and hail a passing four-wheeled cab. He climbed inside. George ran down the steps and, when the vehicle was almost parallel, plunged out into the street. He dragged open the door of Austin's cab and scrambled inside. He crouched on the edge of the seat.

"The Continental Bank has a new customer," he said.

"How did it go?" he asked eagerly.

Austin smiled with a trace of vanity.

"The Continental Bank has a new customer," he said. He was the same slick con-man beneath the bluff disguise.

Austin shook his head. "The laxity of British banking methods is astounding," he said.

"What happened?" George asked.

"I spoke to the manager, giving my name as Charles Johnson Horton, an American manufacturer," Austin grinned at the recollection.

"Yes?"

"I pretended to have inside information on certain City matters, such as the recent closure of Bowles Brothers. This so impressed the guardian of the Continental Bank that he welcomed me as a customer immediately." Austin leaned back, giving a bark of laughter.

"I presented no references and gave the Charing Cross Hotel as my address."

"Astonishing, but convenient," George said. "We can syphon funds from the Bank of England into the new account by checks from Mr. Warren."

Sharply, Austin looked at his brother.

"That's an extremely subtle idea," he said admiringly.

George Bidwell leaned forward and shouted to the driver. "Driver," he yelled. "Stop at the nearest post office. I have a cable to dispatch," he said.

George turned to his brother.

"We must have a fourth man to withdraw the cash from this new account. We will set him up as Mr. Horton's confidential clerk," he said.

Ten minutes later George Bidwell dispatched a telegram to Edwin Noyes, an old friend of Austin's from Hartford, Connecticut. The cable said:

COME WEDNESDAY STEAMER ATLANTIC WITHOUT FAIL

"Which gives my unfortunate friend only two days in which to make his preparations," Austin protested ruefully.

On December 17th Austin and Macdonnell stood by the ticket barrier at Euston Station, peering down the platform. It was sparsely lit and almost deserted; small groups of porters in dark brown corduroys were watching for the boat train.

The station clock said 9 p.m. when the giant green engine *Apollo* appeared at the far end of the line. It nosed purposefully forward up the platform until it reached the buffers and let off an exultant spurt of steam. Immediately the train burst open. Passengers erupted out of carriage doors, porters stepped forward to unclip the luggage vans, engine-driver and firemen climbed off the footplate.

A lightly built man with thick fair hair disentangled himself from the scrum and walked casually to the barrier. Austin spotted him immediately. He carried a hat and single valise, his overcoat was unbuttoned. Edwin Noyes possessed the same boyish face and deceptively vague behavior that attracted Austin to him fifteen years earlier at the McGraw Street Boys' School. His face broke into a wide grin when Austin hailed him. They greeted each other enthusiastically, Macdonnell was introduced, they scooped up a taxi and drove through the gaslit streets to the Grosvenor. Room 94 had been reserved in the name of Brooks. Noyes was shown up to the room to wash and change before starting out for a celebration dinner at the Langham.

Noyes unclipped his bag and took out his dress suit. It was crumpled but new and had been bought with funds sent by Austin a month ago. He pulled Austin's accompanying letter from the inside pocket of the case and skimmed through it while he began to change his clothes.

Grosvenor Hotel, London, November 8, 1872
My dear Noyes,

You will be surprised to hear from me from London, but the fact is I have been here with George and a friend of ours for a year, and have made a lot of money from several speculations we have embarked on. In fact, we have been so successful we have determined to make you a present of a thousand dollars, which find enclosed. Please accept the same with our best wishes.

We may be able to give you a chance to make a few thousands, if you would care to venture across the ocean, perhaps we can make use of you. If so, I will send you a cable. If I do, come anyway as we will pay all your expenses should you determine not to go in with us on the deal. Be cautious and preserve absolute secrecy when you leave home as to your destination. Will explain the reason for this when we meet.

Hoping you are quite well, I remain, etc., etc.

Austin

Noyes washed hastily and brushed his thick mop of hair. It would certainly be interesting to hear details of the Bidwells' plan.

George Bidwell was waiting in the anteroom of a private dining-room at the Langham. He looked cheerful and relaxed. A secret can be an encumbrance until it is told, and the small syndicate had found it increasingly frustrating over the past months to be unable to boast of their inspired plans to anyone.

Confidently, George shook hands with Noyes and led him between marble pillars and potted aspidistras into the dining-room. The room was paneled and the seating covered in red tasseled cushioning.

An excellent dinner was served: hors-d'œuvres, soupe au choux, soles au gratin, ris de veau en caisse, perdreaux Poeles, mutton à la Provençale, aubergines, salad, nougats à la crème. The waiters, after handing round coffee and brandy, withdrew. The diners were alone.

No one spoke for a moment, but the atmosphere was electric with anticipation.

"You tell him, George," Austin said generously.

Bidwell put down the glass he was warming in his hand. He smiled across at Noyes.

"Do not imagine we would drag you across the Atlantic on a fool's errand," he said. "We are on to a tremendous scheme."

"Tremendous," Austin echoed.

"We have worked on it incessantly for four months and achieved considerable success. Now our plan is almost complete." George took a sip of brandy, and continued: "We plan to work the coup for six weeks in the New Year and leave the country by March 1st. With us we will carry funds to keep us in luxury for the rest of our lives."

Noyes was impressed, but he possessed a straightforward mind.

"And what will my work consist of?" he asked.

"Withdrawing all moneys from the bank," George said. "We reckon to give you five per cent on everything you take away."

"And how much do you plan to take away?"

George Bidwell's face flushed dull red.

"£100,000," he said.

Noyes gasped.

"Wherever will it come from?" he asked.

"The Bank of England."

Horrified, Noyes stared across the coffee-cups at Bidwell.

"We have by the tail the greatest financial institution in the world," Austin crowed.

"I have arranged the most elaborate precautions to cover you," George assured him.

Noyes did not speak. He was a small-time forger, a

fringe criminal, who had done time in New Jersey State Prison. Foresight and caution were not among his attributes, but he was overcome by the thought of crossing swords with the Bank of England.

The Bidwells and Macdonnell were astonished at his lack of applause for their plan. Perhaps they should explain more fully. They did, but Noyes remained numb and silent.

The Bidwells exchanged apprehensive glances. They must not allow Noyes to refuse to go in with them. Men they could trust were rare in their line of business.

Austin finished his brandy and got up.

"We must give Ed time to think our project over," he said. He gripped his friend by the shoulder. "Why, you have been traveling for eleven days." He escorted Noyes back to Grosvenor and to bed.

The next day Austin and Macdonnell conducted him on a tour of London. By evening he appeared more relaxed as they led him down the Haymarket.

The wide thoroughfare blazed with light as proprietors clipped back the shutters of oyster bars, coffee houses and drinking dens which lined the pavements. Austin and Macdonnell exchanged derisive pleasantries with prostitutes and pimps who hailed them at street corners, fobbed off rogues and drug peddlers, repelled vendors of oranges, flowers, pencils, knives and doughnuts.

From the moment the three men paid their admission and walked down the narrow passageway into the Turkish Divan they knew they had chosen well. Music and a riot of voices billowed through bead curtains. The saloon was all gilt and red plush, eighty feet square, and packed with humanity. The bar had been serving drinks all day and the atmosphere was thick with cigar smoke. On a platform a small orchestra sawed out the latest giddy waltz.

A man took their coats and Austin led the way between tables and dance floor to a long mahogany bar.

He looked at the barmaids carefully. There were six or seven of them, all extremely pretty, but it was their breasts and the new-style dresses which held his attention. Necklines were cut wide, or plunging to a "V," the opening filled with a chemisette of lace or net. Austin elbowed his way opposite the best pair of bosoms.

"Three sherry cobblers," he demanded. His eyes followed the curve of a long smooth throat to the provocative little face above. Ten minutes later Austin had persuaded Frances Grey to dance.

The evening barmaids at the Turkish Divan were encouraged to fraternize with rich customers, and afterward Frances Grey picked up a tray of drinks and pattered up the balcony stairs to join Austin at his table. He rose and introduced Macdonnell, who kissed the girl's hand with a flourish. She giggled appreciatively.

"He is my doctor," Austin said severely. "Attending in an official capacity this evening."

"I prescribe complete rest," Macdonnell said. He pulled out a chair beside him. "Come and talk to me, Miss Grey," he said.

Frances Grey sat down between them.

"Who is your other friend?" she asked.

Noyes was hunched in his chair, staring blankly out across the dancers.

"He seems ever so serious," she said.

"That's because he is an inventor," Macdonnell told her.

"What's he inventing?"

Macdonnell shouted with laughter. "A machine for milking cows!" He always enjoyed his own jokes best.

During the day Edwin Noyes had convinced himself it would be suicide to go in with the Bidwells. But now at the Turkish Divan he was hit by despair. If he turned down this opportunity what would he do? He had only recently left prison. He was a jailbird, without a profession, unskilled even in felony. Where would he go?

To his home, to a beloved father fighting desperately to stave off bailiffs from his property? To relations, all living on the bread-line? The brutal facts unrolled before him like a dirty newspaper. There was, in fact, no decision to be made.

Austin nodded to Macdonnell.

"Why not take Fanny down to dance," he asked quietly.

When they had gone he shifted over next to Noyes.

"Quite a find, this place," he said amicably.

"Yes."

Austin fiddled with his cigar. He did not speak again, but waited like a cat at a hole. All at once a shudder swept through Noyes. He drew back his shoulders, picked up his glass and swallowed the alcohol.

"How do you plan to get £100,000 out of the country?" he asked.

"In United States bonds," Austin said.

Noyes asked another question, and another, and Austin answered with crisp, concise replies. When Macdonnell rejoined them five minutes later Noyes looked up at him grimly.

"I will come in with you," he said. "I need the money badly."

Austin could not suppress a smug smile of triumph. He stood up.

"It's time for bed," he said, conducting his companions out of the Divan and into a cab.

"I'll walk back," he told them. "I need some exercise."

But Austin was waiting on the curb when Frances Grey left the side entrance of the Turkish Divan twenty minutes later. He stepped forward and gripped her arm.

"Let me take you home," he implored.

Fanny was tired and it was raining. She agreed.

They drove through the dark streets to 80 Tachbrook Street and went upstairs to her room.

Edwin Noyes breakfasted early at the Grosvenor. He could find neither Austin nor Macdonnell, so he fetched his overcoat, deciding to go out alone. Halfway down the palatial staircase to the foyer he saw George Bidwell waiting below. The dour figure stood motionless, his steely eyes regarding him with unblinking disinterest. Noyes descended the stairs and crossed over.

"Good morning." George lifted his mat briefly. "We have a few calls to make this morning. To fit you for the part you have to play."

Without waiting for an answer, George turned and marched out through the swing doors. Noyes followed, gaining little comfort from the thought that his future was inevitably linked with this strange character.

George bundled Noyes into a cab which stopped outside 87 Regent Street.

"Go into Messrs. Kino," George instructed him. "Give your name as Brooks and order two linen shirts and a cheap, navy blue suit."

When they visited Messrs. Bax, hatters in the Strand, George introduced Noyes personally as Mr. Brooks.

Noyes walked out wearing an inconspicuous brown bowler and with a rolled umbrella held awkwardly in one hand.

"Umbrellas are part of an Englishman's uniform," George explained. "They are carried tightly furled in dry weather."

George stopped on the pavement, lifting his top-hat formally.

"That is sufficient for today," he said. "You will be instructed in your duties when the clothes are made."

George strode off alone down the street. Now his mind was busy formulating a plan which would avoid the necessity of Austin having to present forged bills in person at the Western Branch.

7

HAPPY CHRISTMAS,
COLONEL FRANCIS!

A chilling rain spattered against the windows, but inside
the manager's parlor at the Western Branch of the Bank
of England it was warm and secure. A fire burned in the
grate; sprigs of holly perched on the marble mantelshelf, greeting cards crowding the space between. The
rest of the room was polished and immaculate, except
for a puddle of water that was spreading across the floorboards beneath the hatstand where Austin had hung his
dripping raincoat and umbrella.

It was December 23rd, and Mr. Warren had come to
present the compliments of the season to Colonel
Francis. The Colonel was a vital pawn in the game; it
was essential to keep him sympathetic. Beneath the exchange of pleasantries, Austin Bidwell regarded the
Colonel warily. The real purpose of his visit was to ask
a favor. He began to choose his words carefully.

"Unhappily I will be seeing less of you in the New
Year, Colonel," he said. "I have to be in Birmingham
to locate a site for my Pullman Palace sleeping-car
factory. It is amazingly hard to find suitable accommodation in Birmingham and until I find a permanent address perhaps you would forward my mail to the post
office where it is certain to reach me?"

"With pleasure, Mr. Warren." The Colonel picked
up a pencil, leaned forward and made a note on his
tear-off pad.

"Temporary address in New Year, c/o Post Office,
Birmingham," he wrote. The Colonel ripped the note

off his pad, and opened Mr. Warren's file which lay on the desk in front of him. Austin watched with the utmost apprehension. Would the Colonel notice one of the hundred little points in the file which required explanation? The Colonel placed the note inside the front cover of the file and closed it again. Austin braced himself to ask the vital question. He must keep the tone cool and businesslike. Better make it a statement rather than a query.

"Early in the New Year bills of exchange will be arriving from my customers in Europe to pay for the Pullman cars they have ordered," he said. "It will not always be convenient to deliver the bills in person while I am in Birmingham. I will therefore send them through the post in registered letters."

Austin watched a crease of anxiety grow between the Colonel's friendly eyes.

"You realize, Mr. Warren," he said severely, "it is the Bank of England's policy only to discount the very best paper?"

"All my bills of exchange will be acceptable by leading discount houses," Austin assured him hurriedly.

The Colonel did not answer at once. Thoughtfully he stared down at his nails. At length he said:

"If they are the very best paper we will discount them for you."

Austin had won. He got up and shook the Colonel warmly by the hand.

"Goodbye, and a very merry Christmas, Colonel."

"And a successful New Year, Mr. Warren," the Colonel replied.

"I hope so, I sincerely hope so," Austin said, as he strode out of the manager's parlor.

When he reached the pavement Austin hailed a passing cab. Inside he lay back and closed his eyes, a smile of contempt curled his thin mouth. What an idiot he had made of Colonel Francis!

If the Colonel's suspicions were never roused by Mr. Warren as a man his file gave ample clues to the real situation. This mysterious American who was receiving special discount facilities at the Bank of England had no one to vouch for him except a tailor along the street. The tailor could tell the bank that he had known Mr. Warren for the period of one month.

If the bank had shown the slightest concern over Mr. Warren's address cursory inquiries would have revealed that he never slept in his room at the Golden Cross Hotel. Although Mr. Warren's capital was small, there was ample evidence that he frequently sold bills of exchange at quite substantial losses only a few days after purchasing them. Now the bank was prepared to discount bills of exchange sent through the post from Birmingham.

Even more astonishing was the fact that Austin was disconnecting himself completely from Mr. Warren. A dummy figure was left to take responsibility for what Austin hoped would develop into a £100,000 deficit in the Bank of England's reserves.

The cab turned south out of Oxford Street into a side-street.

"This will do excellently," Austin shouted to the driver. It was only a few paces to the little Swiss chocolate shop which Austin frequented every day between eleven and twelve o'clock. He nodded a good morning to the fat proprietor. As a cuckoo clock chimed the hour, he strode between the tables to one in the furthest corner of the room.

Austin had barely sat down when the doorbell clanged and she was there. Austin found excitement flooding through him. He had known the girl four months but was continually entranced by her aura of passionate anticipation. The girl flushed with pleasure when she saw Austin. Her silk dress rustled as she moved toward him. A typically English beauty, she had a fine complexion, short features and a wide, generous mouth. She wore a cloak and hood of royal blue, which matched her eyes. They stood, engulfed in each other's presence. Austin put out a hand.

"Come and sit by me," he said tenderly.

She slid into a chair beside him; their fingers intertwined.

"You are beautiful," he whispered. "Would you like hot chocolate, sweetheart?"

"Yes, but I mustn't stay," she said. Austin gave the order.

"Mama thinks I have gone out to buy ribbons," she giggled, but her eyes were troubled.

Jane Devereux was seventeen. She was living in lodgings in Oxford Street with her mother, for she was "coming out" this season. Her relations had clubbed together to launch her into society, believing that her beauty and high spirits would offset her lack of wealth; her father, a colonel, having died unexpectedly, leaving his small family penniless.

The girl had met Austin at a tea-party. She was instantly attracted by his flamboyant charm. He was so exciting and so different. But her family disapproved when he continued his advances and they forbade her to see him again. She was furious.

Her mother and relations refused to explain their aversion to the young American: they were merely suspicious. The Devereuxs were more perceptive than some of the astutest minds in the financial world.

The family's steps to end the association merely intensified the attachment. Jane found the London Season immeasurably enhanced by smuggled letters and secret meetings, combined with the delightful sensation of thwarting her elders.

"I am so afraid that Mama will find out that I am meeting you," Jane said.

"What could she do?" Austin asked.

"Send me away to the country."

Austin stared blankly at the girl. His fingers clung to hers. He could not bear to be without her at this juncture. He depended on her trust. She gave him eyes to see himself not as he knew himself to be but as he would like to be. In a flash he had the answer.

"They won't separate us!" he cried. "We'll get married secretly."

Directly he said it, he knew it was a good idea. A young wife's obvious innocence would avert suspicion from his name when the forgeries were inevitably discovered at the end of March. He squeezed Jane's hand and smiled at her reassuringly.

"But how exciting, Austin," Jane said eagerly. "How could we manage that?"

Austin had almost forgotten his interview at the Western Branch when he walked purposefully into the coffee house off Finsbury Circus later that morning. But his friends were eager for his news. Amicably, Austin sat down astride a tea-chest and re-enacted every detail of the scene with Colonel Francis. At the end he strode into the bar to fetch a bottle of champagne. He opened it and poured some into three glasses.

"I have a special toast," he said. "To my fiancée!"

Macdonnell and George paused with the champagne halfway to their mouths. They stared inquiringly at Austin. What was the fellow up to now?

"Congratulate me!" Austin continued gaily, "I am to be married next week."

His friends glowered at him.

"Is this some kind of a joke?" George asked suspiciously.

"No."

"Then you must be insane," George told him.

"Who is the girl, does she know of your plans?"

"Of course not." Austin was shocked. "She is a colonel's daughter, she trusts me completely."

Macdonnell groaned.

George put down his glass. "You cannot possibly get married at this stage," he said. "You will bring calamity upon us all."

An unexpected emotion swept Austin's face.

"We cannot wait any longer," he said sulkily.

"But you must. You cannot marry until the Bank of England project is successfully completed." George Bidwell spoke crisply and with certainty. Austin knew he was right.

"Now forget about it for a few months," George said. "If the girl is worthwhile she will be happy to wait."

Austin stared moodily into his glass.

"Very well," he said grudgingly. "I will postpone it for the present."

George stared narrowly at his younger brother. He was not reassured by Austin's easy acquiescence. At once he sought a way to separate Austin from temptation.

Meanwhile it was Christmas. George Bidwell issued an invitation. "Nellie and I are pleased to invite you all for Christmas dinner," he said.

Nellie Vernon slipped out on a shopping expedition to Bond Street when she heard she was to be hostess at the celebration. At Bowring and Arundel she bought silk scarves for the men and asked to have them embroidered with initials. She chose gloves for the ladies who were to join the party after dinner.

Edwin Noyes was introduced to Nellie as Mr. Howe from Liverpool when she and the four conspirators sat down to dinner in a private room of Ford's Hotel, Manchester Square. It was 1 a.m., when Austin, Macdonnell and Noyes, each with a girl on his arm, stepped noisily into the deserted square. The long months of preparation were over, they were replete in mind and body, the future was bathed in gold.

8

OFF
THE TRACKS

The excitement of all perfected plans carries an element of dread. For action is called for, and action long anticipated is often hard to begin. The merry bells of Christmas 1872 sounded a little hollow to George Bidwell. Soon he knew that he must gamble not only his precious plans but his liberty as well, in one decisive move. His horror of final commitment was dispersed into a thousand little fears; his meticulous mind ferreted out endless small tasks still to be completed and essential precautions to be taken.

First the fraud machine must be tested. While Austin and Macdonnell chafed with impatience, George performed a kind of dress rehearsal to convince himself that the British banking system was really as naive as it appeared.

On December 28th he took the train to Birmingham and posted a registered packet to Colonel Francis. It contained a letter from Mr. Warren and ten bills of exchange totalling £4,307. George waited in Birmingham two days and then picked up, from the post office, a letter from Colonel Francis informing Mr. Warren that the bills had been satisfactorily discounted to him. This was not surprising, for the bills were genuine and drawn on leading European financial houses. George caught the next train back to London. He had tested his fraud machine; it was working perfectly.

Next he studied his brother's position, which would be extremely vulnerable directly the forgeries began to reach the Western Branch. Austin required a cast-iron alibi. After two days, though, George surfaced with an inspired solution. He would pack Austin off to America before the coup began. Austin would not only be safe from the law but removed from the temptation of matrimonial entanglement.

With Austin taken care of, Noyes had to be considered. He would be handling all withdrawals from Mr. Horton's account and must also be protected. At Bidwell's suggestion Noyes put an advertisement in the *Daily Telegraph* which was to establish him as a stranger to Mr. Horton.

A gentleman of active business habits seeks a situation of trust or partnership. Address particulars to Edwin Noyes, Durrant's Hotel, Manchester Square.

One evening before the advertisement appeared in print Noyes arrived at Durrant's Hotel without any luggage and booked Room No. 2 for the price of twelve shillings a week. Nearly sixty letters arrived for Noyes at Durrant's Hotel during the week of January 6th–11th when the advertisement was running in the *Telegraph*. One was from Mr. C. J. Horton.

Noyes was breakfasting in the coffee-room one morning when Austin was shown in. Noyes rose from his chair and the two men shook hands.

"I am Mr. Horton," Austin spoke loudly to ensure that the staff would overhear. "And I am looking for a confidential clerk."

Noyes said he was available and outlined his past experience in a quiet nervous voice. Horton asked a few questions, received satisfactory replies, and decided that Noyes would do very well.

"If you will accompany me to my solicitor, Mr. Noyes," Horton said, "we will have a formal agreement drawn up."

In the dingy office of David Howell, solicitor, of 105

Cheapside, the contract "between Charles Johnson Horton of London Bridge Hotel Manufacturer and Edwin Noyes of Durrant's Hotel Merchant's Clerk" was drawn up and signed.

Noyes agreed to serve as clerk and manager at a salary of £150 a year, and to deposit a sum of £300 as security "for the due performance of his duties and honesty such sum to be returned without interest on his leaving."

George Bidwell instructed Noyes to carry this agreement and a copy of the *Daily Telegraph* advertisement with him everywhere. They would serve to establish his innocence should the need arise.

Edwin Noyes was suitably clothed and protected. Next morning Austin took him on a duty tour of the City. They called at the Terminus Hotel, London Bridge, and booked a private sitting-room, No. 6, to serve as an office. Mr. Horton introduced his clerk to the manager of the Continental Bank, explaining that in future Noyes would be acting for him in every way.

"I wish you to treat Mr. Noyes as you would myself," he said. The manager looked surprised.

"In that case would you allow him to sign checks?" he asked.

"Most certainly not," Austin snapped.

Noyes smiled wryly. He was amused by Austin's transformation into a raw-mannered Yankee.

The last call of the day was to Jay, Cooke McCulloch, large American bankers in Lombard Street, who specialized in placing U.S. bonds on the market. Here Noyes was again introduced as Mr. Horton's clerk and instructed in the details of U.S. bond-buying. Austin and Noyes then reported back to George—"The stage is set."

This information served only to intensify the crisis through which George was passing. The last straw was a letter he received one morning from his wife. She wrote of the difficulties of living alone with a young child and implored him to return home to the States.

With uncharacteristic impetuosity George Bidwell drove straight to the Grosvenor Hotel and burst into Austin's room. Briefly he informed his half-dressed brother that he had decided to drop the Bank of England project and return to Chicago to engage in trade. Austin stared at him incredulously.

"You cannot back out at this late stage," he objected.

Macdonnell sat bolt upright in bed.

"In heaven's name why?" he asked.

George glanced coldly at Macdonnell. He did not intend to explain the agonizing pangs of conscience he had been suffering. George had been reared on strict religious principles and complete honesty, but his parents had been desperately poor. George Bidwell's earlier excursions into crime had provided money to send his younger brothers and sisters to school. But the Bank of England project was impelled not by necessity but through greed.

George pulled out a small black notebook and turned the pages.

"I figure we have £6,300 remaining," he said. "I would therefore be glad if you would withdraw £2,100 from the Western Branch this morning, which is my share."

Austin swallowed. "Well, certainly, George," he said ingratiatingly. "But come now, there isn't all that hurry."

Sharply, George looked up at him.

"There certainly is," he said. "I am catching the transatlantic steamer from Liverpool tomorrow."

George brushed aside their objections.

"I have no time for argument," he said. He turned the handle of the door. "I will return at noon for my capital."

He hurried off down the corridor to complete his preparations for departure.

At noon the wily Austin greeted his brother coolly.

"We will be sorry to see you go, George," he said, "but in the circumstances we would be much obliged if you'd leave your capital in our hands."

George Bidwell's cold eyes widened.

"We will require to use it," Austin said.

George Bidwell considered his friends anxiously. They were lounging in easy chairs, and no longer appeared worried. With a shock he realized that Austin and Macdonnell intended to carry out the coup without him. His beloved plans bungled by two reckless idiots! The appalling thought brought him sharply to his senses.

"I have been unable to obtain a passage to the States immediately," he said carefully. "I will therefore be remaining a few more days."

"Good, very good," Austin murmured.

George Bidwell accepted a chair and a cigarette, his agitation slowly simmered down.

During lunch, which was sent up to the room, George admitted that there was one more point on which he required confirmation. Despite Austin's repeated assurances that Mr. Warren's credit at the bank was solid as a rock, George could not believe that Colonel Francis was completely fooled. He felt that a final show of respectability was needed, proof that Mr. Warren had influence in high places.

"I would like you to go to Paris, Austin," he said, "and procure a bill of exchange on Rothschilds."

Austin threw down his napkin.

"You are quite impossible, George," he said disgustedly. "The Rothschilds straddle Europe, they are famed for their exclusiveness."

"Exactly," George replied.

Austin ran his hand through his hair.

"Very well, then, I will see what I can do," he said. "But we start active operations directly I return."

On Sunday, January 12th, Austin boarded the boat

train at Victoria. His wallet was bulging with francs, but his mind lacked inspiration for a way to accomplish his mission.

"I expect an expense of a thousand dollars, a delay of two weeks, and nothing accomplished at the end," he grumbled.

Austin was a bad sailor and suffered appallingly on the cross-channel steamer. At half past midnight he arrived at Calais and boarded the train to Paris. He paid ten francs extra for a *coupé*, stretched himself full length on the hard seat and fell asleep.

The next thing he knew he was being hurled across the compartment. As his shoulder hit the opposite wall with a crack, Austin flung his arms round his head. The carriage groaned and squealed, heeled over and crashed on to the embankment. Austin fell with it.

It was pitch dark, but he seemed to be alive. His arms and hands had been cut by flying glass. He tried to move his legs; they were trapped. The roof of the carriage was lying across his knees. Austin hoisted himself into a sitting position. He began to drag at the roof with his hands, it shifted an inch and the carriage door came tumbling down on top of him. Surprise snapped Austin's jangled nerves. Frantically he began to yell for help.

At Marquise Station they heard the crash. The station master and guard jumped down off the platform and began to run over the sleepers, their oil hurricane lamps flickering as they ran. They found the engine had ploughed off the rails; the tender, luggage van and two coaches were lying in a heap on the embankment. The driver and fireman were dead, the stoker was hideously injured, screaming passengers were trapped in the wreckage.

Austin was prised loose and lifted on to a stretcher. In the station waiting-room he was given first aid, a blanket and a mug of black coffee laced with brandy. Glumly, Austin stared round at his fellow sufferers. He

cursed his luck and his brother even more. Idly, he began to decipher the notices printed in French across the
walls: "It is forbidden to spit. By order of the President, Chemin de Fer du Nord." A bell of recollection
clanged in Austin's head. Who was the President of this
railway? He had it—Baron Alphonse Rothschild, the
man he wished to interview.

Excitedly, Austin fumbled in his overcoat pocket with
his bandaged hand. He pulled out a small leather-bound
notebook and began to thumb through it. The notebook
was filled with details of the Rothschilds, compiled by
George.

1764, Mayer Rothschild sets up as second-hand
dealer in Frankfurt ghetto.

Austin flicked the page.

1846, James Rothschild open Chemin de Fer du
Nord, gigantic project linking Paris with industrial
north. Cheers from Crown, President and all
France. Three weeks after opening, train rounded
a bend too fast and thirty-seven passengers killed.
Cheers revert to violent anti-Semitic storm. Rothschild lampooned in Press, jeered at in the streets.
Rothschilds sensitive thereafter concerning train
derailments.

Austin closed the little book. The information had
been very helpful.

It was noon before Austin could persuade himself to
board another train. He reached Paris by nightfall and
drove to the Grand Hôtel in the Boulevard des Capu-
cines, where he spent a restless night.

At 10 a.m. next morning Austin climbed out of a
carriage in the Rue Lafitte. He limped in through the
unpretentious entrance of Maison Rothschild. The

façade was a blind. From the courtyard inside, Austin looked upon a palace which had originally been owned by Napoleon's Commissioner of Police, Marshal Fouche. He caught a glimpse through tall windows of gilt-framed pictures and fine antique furniture. Austin turned in to a door marked "English Department" and crossed to the largest desk in the room.

Mr. Gatley, head of the English Department, blotted the signature he had written and looked up at the figure standing by his desk and leaning heavily on a cane. He raised his eyes over the perfectly tailored black suit, the new tie, the face . . .

"What in heaven's name have you been doing to yourself, sir?" Mr. Gatley asked. He turned to the clerk standing by his elbow. "Fetch a seat immediately for this gentleman, please, de Lorelli," he said.

Austin was glad to sit down. A little color slid back into his ashen cheeks. His whole face was swollen and striped with plaster, his leg throbbed painfully. Austin glanced round the tables to be sure he had an audience.

"I have been in a train accident on the Chemin de Fer du Nord," he said.

A gasp of anxiety swept the room.

"The Marquise disaster?" Mr. Gatley asked.

Austin nodded. He lifted a bandaged hand and touched his face nervously.

"I was trapped in the wreckage for half an hour, it has affected my nerves greatly," he said pathetically.

"But how terrible!" said Mr. Gatley. "Baron Rothschild will be very distressed to hear you have suffered so greatly. If there is anything at all we can do to help."

"I am in no condition to transact the business I came to do in Paris, I will return to London immediately," Austin said.

"I think that might be advisable," Gatley agreed paternally.

"I wish to transfer certain funds back to London,"

Austin continued. "It would greatly assist me if you would draw a three-monthly bill for me on your London house for £4,500."

Mr. Gatley paused. He shook his head sadly.

"It is not our custom to give long paper," he said. "I am afraid I must refuse your request."

"Oh, how very distressing!" Austin gasped. He was genuinely close to tears. He staggered to his feet. Mr. Gatley bit his lip in agitation. You never could tell, the Baron might be prepared to make an exception in the circumstances.

"If you will return at noon," Mr. Gatley said comfortingly, "I will see if something can be done to accommodate you."

Austin Bidwell was back on the doorstep as the ormulu clock in the English Department struck twelve. A small middle-aged man was standing squarely on the carpet conversing with Mr. Gatley. His stomach protruded roundly beneath a gold watchchain, he wore a flower in his buttonhole, he was stroking one of his handsome moustaches with long fingers. Austin stared with fascination at the face. A pair of canny brown eyes, a long curving nose, a strong relentless chin. This was the Baron Alphonse de Rothschild, the man who had recently arbitrated peace between France and the Prussians.

Introduced to the Baron as Mr. Warren, Austin supplied an eyewitness account of the train crash and explained what he required. When he said goodbye he had obtained Rothschild's signature to a bill of exchange for 113,000 francs 50 centimes. With the aid of a fortuitous train accident it had taken less than two days to complete an almost impossible mission.

Austin was one of those happy men who could turn even disaster to advantage once he had set his mind on a definite end. He stopped off at the post office and dispatched a cable to his friends:

THE EGYPTIANS ALL PASSED OVER THE RED SEA
BUT THE HEBREWS WERE DROWNED THEREIN.

Thirty-six hours later Austin was back in London.

Next morning, Friday, January 17th, accompanied
by Macdonnell, he drove to the Western Branch. The
genuine Rothschild bill was folded carefully into his
wallet, while Macdonnell had several duplicates in his
possession. With commendable foresight Austin had
visited the stationer's close to the Rue Lafitte and procured blank bill forms of the cheap blue paper identical
to that used by the Rothschilds. Macdonnell had filled
in the blanks.

Austin hobbled into the Colonel's parlor. He explained his battered condition.

"I had a bad fall from my horse while hunting in
Warwickshire," Austin told him. "I am down from
Birmingham for a few days to consult my doctor, so
I thought I would take this opportunity to call upon
you."

The Colonel expressed appropriate regret at the accident.

"I have been offered three factory sites in Birmingham," Austin said. "We expect to start production of
the Pullman cars by February. My financial transactions
will be much larger and many more bills of exchange
will be coming in."

The Colonel raised an eyebrow. The Pullman car
project was wearing a little thin and he was beginning to
wonder what Mr. Warren was actually up to.

"Providing your bills of exchange are first-class paper
there should be no difficulty," he said coldly.

Austin Bidwell slid the Rothschild bill from his wallet
and dropped it on to the Colonel's desk.

"I suppose that is good enough paper?" he asked with
studied casualness.

Colonel Francis was impressed. If the Rothschilds
were backing Mr. Warren's Pullman cars all must be

well. He looked across at his young customer with new interest. Lionel Rothschild, head of the London branch, was one of the twenty-four directors of the Bank of England.

The Colonel had no opportunity to ingratiate himself with his client, for Mr. Warren never visited the Western Branch again. His part in the conspiracy was over.

Next morning Austin boarded the boat train at Victoria. He was traveling via Calais to Le Havre to pick up a transatlantic liner. George accompanied him on the first leg of the journey. He wanted to be sure that Austin left the country without the girl who might subvert his good sense. At Calais he waited to see Austin's luggage stowed on board the boat train to Le Harve before wishing him goodbye.

Affectionately, Austin watched his brother climb back up the gang-plank of the cross-channel packet to face the hazards of carrying out the Bank of England coup. He was delighted not to be going with him. He was free to do what he wanted.

When he saw the small, black-sided steamer reverse from its Calais berth and chug out of the harbor toward Dover he called a porter to transfer his luggage from the Le Harve boat train to the Paris express. On his own initiative, and without reference to his brother whom he knew would be against the project, Austin was making some adjustments to his program. He had decided to marry Jane Devereux in Paris and take her with him to the States. It was a decision conceived during the agony of parting from Jane in London. Austin shrugged off the knowledge that the move was reckless and ill-advised. He wanted Jane Devereux and did not believe in thwarting his desires.

George Bidwell, Macdonnell and Noyes, left behind in London, were an ill-assorted trio. Austin had been the link and leavening influence between them all. But now the knowledge that they were bound together in a common purpose overcame their differences of temperament and thought. The decision to go ahead had been made. There was nothing to do but make the best of it.

During the next three days the syndicate made preparations for a speedy get away in case the forgeries did not go through. George changed £1,300 to francs in case they needed to go into hiding on the Continent. Noyes emptied the two bank accounts to ensure that no further capital would be lost if the banks were sealed against them. They settled all outstanding accounts and packed everything except their daily needs.

It was almost with relief that George Bidwell boarded the early train to Birmingham on January 21st with three forged bills in his pocket.

9

GOLD
IN THE STREETS

The forged bills were posted, there was nothing to do but wait. It would be two nights and a day before a reply came from Colonel Francis to say that the forgeries had been accepted. But would they be accepted? This was the question which nagged at Bidwell's brain during every one of the next forty hours. His whole future turned on a trial of skill between Macdonnell and the anonymous committee of the Bank of England who would examine the bills before passing them for discount.

It was said that old bill brokers could "smell bad paper," but the keenest olfactory nerves might become clogged with disuse. And if the bills were as perfect as Macdonnell claimed the odor might be faint enough to miss. This was the thin premise on which the conspirators built all their hopes.

Driven from his private suite at the Queen's Hotel by the perishing cold, George Bidwell sought refuge in the coffee-room. It was dark and cheerless as a mammoth's cave but he spied a tiny fire in the distance, smoldering resentfully in the blackened grate. Striding across the room, he slipped into a frosty leather armchair and picked up the poker, stabbing the coal into flame. He sat back and rubbed his hands, pleased with his positive contribution to the scene. Did his fellow guests appreciate his enterprise? He glanced round, they were all men. Half a dozen were fast asleep in their chairs, the rest were obscured from the waist by open newspapers. Except for a man beside him. George swiveled around to examine him. He was square-faced, middle-aged and dressed in chocolate brown. His beard and whiskers were chocolate brown, his eyes, his pipe the same. His gaze was fixed vacantly on a cigarette burn in the carpet at his feet. Only a white curl of smoke rising from his lips confirmed that he was still alive. George Bidwell pursed his lips in irritation, his eyes narrowed in dislike. He detested Englishmen and their self-sufficiency. Their indifference to him was an offense. He smiled thinly. They would notice him when they learned he had ravished their god, the Bank of England.

But suppose the bills of exchange were thrown out, what then? No doubt Colonel Francis would acknowledge them just the same and detectives would be stationed at the post office to arrest Mr. Warren when he arrived to pick up his mail. George would not be so rash as to walk into such a trap. Precautions had been taken.

A cab-driver asked for Mr. Warren's letters at the post office on Thursday morning, January 23rd. Alfred Morley was a familiar figure in the streets of Birmingham, for seven years he had waited at the cab-rank outside the Queen's Hotel ready to drive visiting executives around the town. The post-office clerk handed him Mr. Warren's mail without question, and Morley shuffled out, grumbling sourly over customers who made him run errands while they remained snug in his cab round the corner.

But George Bidwell was not relaxing, he was watching for the police. His eyes were riveted on the street corner, his hand grasped the door handle of the cab, his body was tensed for flight. Noyes had followed up from London that morning and now lingered on the pavement near the cab ready to obstruct, with seeming innocence, George's possible pursuers.

But the driver turned the corner alone and clambered

up to his seat. He drove the short distance to the station with the letter stuffed casually into his coat pocket.

George had timed it well. As the cab drew up at the station putdown, he leapt out, took the precious letter from the driver and paid him off. He and Noyes sprinted on to the platform and climbed into the London express. A few seconds later it steamed out of the station.

George tore open the envelope. The letter from Colonel Francis was businesslike and courteous:

Dear Sir,

  Your favor of the 21st enclosing £4,250 in bills for discount is received and the proceeds of the same passed to your credit as requested. Hoping you are recovering from the effects of the fall from your horse and that I may have the pleasure of seeing you in London soon, I remain, dear sir,

Yours faithfully,
P. M. Francis

George read it through, stared at it a second, and handed it to Noyes.

"We've done it!" he said with satisfaction.

The invincible shrine of established society had cracked before his wits and ingenuity. George Bidwell's innate sense of superiority was justified.

"My God," Noyes breathed, "we are all rich men!" A wave of relief and happiness engulfed them.

Arriving in London, Noyes drove straight to the City to retrieve the prize. He stopped a messenger in Lombard Street, asking him to cash a £5 check at the Continental Bank. When the messenger returned unscathed, Noyes penetrated the bank in person. He transferred the cash from the forgeries out of Mr. Warren's account at the Bank of England by a check in favor of Mr. Horton. The resulting pile in Horton's account he drew in cash with one of Mr. Horton's checks which Austin had signed before he left.

Noyes hurried back to George and Macdonnell with his haul. His friends fingered the banknotes delightedly. It was incredible! The Bank of England was giving away money!

The Bank of England was the absent host at their festivities that night. During the celebrations George proposed a toast to the continuing good health of a corporation which had so generously exchanged £4,000 in cash that day for three worthless bits of paper.

Austin waited anxiously in France for Macdonnell to tell him the news. He was living in Paris in a style befitting a friend of the Rothschilds and a customer of the Bank of England. He booked into the Hôtel St. James, on the Rue de Rivoli. He hired a four-in-hand and engaged Henry Nunn as groom and personal valet.

Jane and Mrs. Devereux had arrived in Paris. Only two nights ago Mrs. Devereux had been woken by a noise. She had found her child not only dressed but packing. The ensuing scene of defiance and revolt had ended in a mutual storm of tears. Mrs. Devereux had swallowed her forebodings and agreed to accompany Jane to Paris to be a witness to her marriage.

Superficially, Austin was an excellent host. Over the years he had learned to cloak the ruthless inner core of his personality with wit and charm. But anxiety about the forgeries was harder to disguise. As Tuesday slid irrevocably into Wednesday, and Wednesday into Thursday, Austin began to flag.

That morning Austin had arranged an outing to Versailles and booked lunch at the best hotel. By three o'clock it was obvious the expedition was a failure. Austin's powers of conversation had evaporated as he struggled with the fear that he would have to alter all his plans and disappear in haste. He fidgeted, he could not eat, repeatedly he glanced down into the cobbled courtyard from his vantage seat beside the window. Henry Nunn had been left behind in Paris to receive Macdonnell's cable. At last he saw his man turn in through the wrought-iron gates. The telegram his servant carried ran:

ALL WELL BOUGHT AND SHIPPED FORTY BALES MAC

Fortune had smiled on Austin Bidwell once again. He laughed delightedly. Young, rich and in love, he held all the tricks in the game.

Austin lifted his glass.

"To a business venture successfully promoted—and the ladies," he smiled.

Jane responded thankfully to Austin's change of mood.

"To Austin," she said.

Mrs. Devereux was touched by the sight of her daughter's infatuation for the rather over-confident American. Her suspicions were lulled, though not extinguished, by his generosity and obvious delight.

That evening Austin wrote to George. He proffered hearty congratulations and enclosed a wedding invitation for February 8th at the American Embassy in Paris.

In London his brother was forcing the pace now that the coup was under way. Next morning he was a passenger on the early train to Birmingham.

The first batch of bills merely covered their expenses. He was eager now to show a profit and prove to himself that what had been accomplished once could be repeated again and again. On January 24th, he dispatched from Birmingham eight forged bills totaling £9,850. Two of these were made out on cheap blue paper and had Rothschild's marked as the acceptors. George had artfully arranged that a stream of genuine bills from Mr. Warren's file were falling due and being honored at the same time that the forgeries were coming in. The bank happily discounted this second lot of bills.

Mr. Warren had been absent from the scene for seven days and during this time £14,000 had been paid into his account from Bank of England funds. On the journey back from Birmingham, George methodically partitioned out the cash. £4,250 took care of the expenses, and five per cent for Noyes dispatched another £700, leaving £9,100 to be divided equally among the principals.

The plan was undoubtedly a success. Their dream had achieved reality and riches unlimited lay at their feet. Macdonnell's reaction to this good fortune was typically bizarre. He took his umbrella to be re-covered at a hatter's in the Strand. Noyes ordered another suit for the princely sum of £3 10s. and George went to be measured for a black hunting coat, striped waistcoat and Bedford cord breeches at Messrs. Newton of Hanover Square.

A few days later two registered packets were dispatched to the States. One contained £2,000 which Macdonnell had borrowed from his father to set up in Wall Street as a broker. The other held £1,000 to dispose of Noyes' debt and straighten out the finances of his family. A letter was enclosed:

Dear Bro. Johnnie,

I have this day registered a letter to you via John W. Nixon of Naval Office Custom House, New York City, containing £1,000 sterling, which you will collect to best advantage. After you collect it, carry $1,400 over to Charles to pay Smith $750 and also he will pay that bond of 600 that father owes Henry Kennedy for that woodland. The bond is endorsed by John Maclean; so you will see that Kennedy will sicken of the prospect of getting a hold of our homestead. Take 250 dollars yourself to buy your wife a 150 dollar sewing machine, a suit of nice clothes for yourself, cotton cloth out of which Leiz will make for herself and mother under-garments, etc. as a present from me. Don't let Cos. Jul or anyone know but that you bought them yourself. Also deduct your and Leiz expenses to go to Springfield and out home. Also hand Robert Chapman 50 dollars if he should want it (I offered to lend him it). Take a receipt for it to pay to father when he can if I am not at home. The balance you may place to my account in the First National Bank, Hartford, subject to be drawn by Leiz in case of death of me or accident or long absence of six months. Say nothing to no one as to my whereabout. It is not certain when I shall return to America. I confess that I am beginning to like to stay in Europe. More anon. next time.

Yours as ever, Ed.

10

RED-HOT BONDS
AND BANKNOTES

Cucumber sandwiches, hot buttered toast and crumpets, followed by thin bread and butter with jam and cake; George Bidwell sat in a chair by the fire enjoying afternoon tea. He and Nellie had changed their lodgings to 87 Grosvenor Place, where the management and servants accepted them without question.

George wiped his moustaches with a lace-trimmed napkin.

"I have work to do, Nellie," he said.

Nellie watched him over the silver teapot as he crossed the room and picked up a case standing by the desk. She stifled an inclination to ask a dozen questions, as he walked into the bedroom.

She knew the case was stuffed with money. She had knocked against it that morning when George was out, and it had fallen open. Bonds and banknotes had poured across the floor. Where did such a quantity of money come from? she had wondered as she stuffed the money back. Now she poured herself another cup of tea, thrusting awful suspicions to the back of her mind.

George was feeling pleased. He had been to Birmingham again and posted forged bills for £11,072. It had doubled their gains. (Their capital now stood, in terms of today's buying power, at the equivalent of £250,000.)

With a fortune already in hand, Bidwell's most urgent consideration was to blot out every clue connecting their names with the fraud. He heaved the case on to the bed and opened it. Noyes had been busy. The eleventh-hour addition to the team had proved a success. George had found Noyes hard-working, obedient, reliable. Bidwell picked up a packet of thousand-dollar bonds and fingered them through. All the bonds had been bought in the name of Horton or Warren. There was no clue there. U.S. bonds had been chosen in preference to other securities because they were easily convertible in the States and unidentifiable. Or were they? Bidwell frowned as he read the number in the righthand corner of the topmost bill—114,864. He flicked to the next one—114,865, and the next—114,866. My God! Each had a separate number, its own identification! And the banknotes, of course they were numbered too. What a fool he had been not to think of it before. The banks would have the numbers noted in Warren and Horton's files. George threw down the packet of bonds. He glared at the mound of plunder. The case was not a treasure chest but a box of clues to disaster. Disgustedly he slammed the lid.

Bidwell knew the forgeries would inevitably be discovered at the end of March when the first forged bill was thrown out by the first alleged acceptor. The Bank of England having been duped, the search for the culprits would be intensive and prolonged. Anyone presenting bonds or banknotes bearing numbers marked down in Horton or Warren's file would instantly be apprehended. Bidwell was roused from these unsavory thoughts by Nellie's shrieks. He went to investigate. Macdonnell had come in and was brandishing a £100 note in front of Nellie's eyes.

"See what I have, Nellie," he teased. "Guess where I got this."

Bidwell's eyes narrowed in dislike. How dare the idiot fool about so dangerously? Nellie's hand shot out.

"It's mine," she cried. "Let me see!"

Macdonnell whipped the note away. He flourished it above his head.

"It's yours for a kiss, Nellie," he bantered. Nellie began to scramble on to a chair.

"That's enough!" Bidwell's voice cut into their laughter. Nellie turned guiltily, stepped down and began to smooth the tassels of her red dress.

"I'd like a word with you, Macdonnell."

"Good afternoon, George. This girl of yours is too inquisitive."

Macdonnell smiled coolly. He folded the note into his pocket, patted Nellie on the behind and crossed to his chief. When the bedroom door had closed, George turned to Mac.

"I have a problem," he said.

Mac furled a long arm around the brass-domed bedrail.

"Good, good," he said.

"All the banknotes we have accumulated are numbered. We dare not present one after March 25th," George said. "Already this case is completely full."

"Full of red-hot bonds and banknotes!" Macdonnell laughed. "A perfect wedding gift for Austin."

George Bidwell's stare did not flicker and a small crease of concentration grew between Macdonnell's eyes.

"I have it," he said, pulling a handful of sovereigns from his trouser pocket. "Gold. Gold is not numbered. Everything must be changed to sovereigns."

George Bidwell smiled thinly.

"A bright notion," he conceded. "But totally impractical. It would take months to change 100,000 banknotes into sovereigns. We have only a few weeks."

"But it must be possible to change large quantities of notes for gold at the Bank of England," Macdonnell insisted. "It is the basis of the entire banking system." His face brightened. "Why, yes, I remember an occasion when Nathan Rothschild . . ."

"Very well," George cut the diversion short. "I will ask Noyes to make inquiries in Threadneedle Street. In the meantime we will take this case to Austin in France as you suggest."

Austin was not overjoyed to receive his brother's telegram.

MEET US CALAIS MIDNIGHT FEBRUARY 7TH GEORGE

He would have to make the tiresome journey from Paris and the meeting would inevitably run over into his wedding morning. But he was waiting on the pierhead when the night packet from Dover tied up. The friends greeted one another warmly and George handed Austin his wedding present. The numbered bonds and banknotes had been concealed in a black leather dressing-case with the Bidwell coat of arms engraved on the lid. Down to the end of the mole they strolled, exchanging news.

"Our next venture together will be legitimate," they agreed. "We will build grain elevators and stockyards out in the prairies, we will be kings of the Middle West."

After his brother and Macdonnell had boarded the cross-channel packet Austin returned to Paris and was married that afternoon at the chapel of the American Embassy. He carefully stage-managed every detail of the ceremony to present a reassuringly official picture. The principal witnesses were Jane's mother, Mrs. Devereux, and E. B. Washburne, Envoy Extraordinary and Minister Plenipotentiary of the United States in Paris. Austin was in high spirits and Jane supremely happy, though her assessment of her husband's character was essentially inaccurate owing to his suppression of certain salient facts. Only Mrs. Devereux had a needling suspicion that all was not as it appeared. She insisted on a settlement for her penniless daughter of £40 and two silk dresses a year.

Two days later Austin and Jane Bidwell were in a first-class carriage on the night train to Madrid. Austin lifted a large picnic basket from the luggage rack and placed it on the vacant seat opposite. He hinged up the table from the carriage door and began spreading out an evening meal of chicken and champagne.

Austin was feeling pleased with himself. He had achieved his aims in business and marriage, despite all opposition, but the strain on his nerves had been severe. Now he and his wife were to spend a ten-day holiday in Spain. From Madrid they would drive by carriage down through the sunny Iberian peninsula to Cadiz and pick up a boat to Mexico. He would be safely hidden in some hacienda in the Mexican hinterland by the end of March, when news of the Bank of England forgeries hit the headlines.

"How clever you are to arrange everything so well!" Jane smiled. She looked happily over her glass of champagne at her husband. Austin smiled back.

Next morning, before breakfast, the Madrid express came to a halt. An insurrection had broken out in northern Spain and during the night Carlist revolutionaries had been ripping up sections of the main line.

Austin found himself marooned at high altitude in the Pyrenees. His wife expressed herself enchanted with the snow-clad peaks and prospects of fresh adventures, but Austin looked grave. He knew that time was not on his side.

At the Issue Department of the Bank of England, Noyes had changed two £500 notes to gold. He visited the Bank of England next day and changed some more. It became a routine duty. Now the embarrassment of having suspect notes and numbered bonds lying around the hotel room was replaced by the inconvenience of stowing away the bags of gold. A thousand sovereigns weigh seventeen and a half pounds, or as much as a well-filled suitcase, and it was obviously impractical to travel any distance with plunder in this form.

Then Noyes discovered it was possible to change sovereigns back to banknotes at the Bank of England.

It would be suspicious if he were to perform both operations, so Macdonnell undertook the new task.

Macdonnell detested mundane duties of this kind. He protested that any venue would be preferable to the Bank of England. But George insisted. Next morning he escorted Macdonnell as far as the Royal Exchange. They were accompanied by a green-uniformed messenger pushing a two-wheeled hand cart. It carried Macdonnell's black tin trunk and was filled with 6,300 gold sovereigns, each one the rightful property of the Bank of England. Macdonnell stared moodily across the roadway. Loaded wagons and carriages obstructed a view of the iron railings of the Bank of England.

Anxiety rose like a growth in his throat, he swallowed it down.

"Forward," he commanded and stepped out to cross the street. Macdonnell swept through the tall, arched entrance and into the great hall of the bank, the handcart trundling behind. It was a magnificent room, perhaps eighty feet long, with a fine fretwork ceiling and a statue of William III at the end. They had reached the hexagonal drinking fountain in the center of the room when a salmon-coated messenger touched Macdonnell on the arm.

"No smoking, if you please, sir," he requested confidentially. Macdonnell dropped his cigar on the flagstones and trod it out.

Reaching the outer office of the weighing-room, he asked the clerk for notes in exchange for gold. The man took his name and the trunk and asked him to wait. Macdonnell sat down on the wooden bench and opened *The Times*. The messenger leaned contentedly against the wall. He was an old soldier used to lengthy pauses in his routine. These messengers were a familiar sight in London at the time, and were stationed on all the main thoroughfares to carry letters, parcels and messages for a moderate fee.

Half an hour later the messenger's head had fallen

forward, he was asleep. Macdonnell was striding up and down. Half an hour to weigh 6,000 sovereigns! The place was either crumbling with decay or he had been discovered. He pulled out his cigar-case for the fourth time and realized he could not smoke.

Macdonnell's gold was causing comment in the weighing-room. Two clerks, the Superintendent and the Principal were grouped around the vertical tubular hopper of one of the ten weighing machines. The machines were small brass boxes operated by steam and incorporating an ingenious mechanism which threw sovereigns of full weight into one bucket and into another those which were slightly light from being passed from hand to hand. There were 5,998 sovereigns in one bucket and only two in the other.

The Principal went out to make inquiries. Macdonnell watched him approach.

"Mr. Macdonnell?"

"Yes," Macdonnell breathed faintly.

"I am Principal of the Issue Department. I would like you to tell me where you got this gold."

Where indeed? Macdonnell swallowed.

"I, er, brought it with me from Lisbon," he lied.

The Principal looked at him sternly. "It is very rare to have so many sovereigns of full weight," he said.

Macdonnell's body relaxed. He smiled widely at the Principal. So it was nothing to do with the forgeries, after all. Only a detail had gone wrong, not the whole business. Another time he would make sure that more of the sovereigns were worn. He had merely ripped open the sealed bags of gold which Noyes had brought from the Bank of England, taken out the checking slips, and poured them into his black tin trunk.

But Mr. Reece Adams continued to question him.

"Did you receive the gold from Knowles and Foster of Lisbon?"

"No, not from Knowles and Foster."

"I could have sworn they were our own sovereigns we had issued ourselves," the Principal persisted.

"Really?"

Mr. Adams stared hard at his customer and turned away. Bank officials were not encouraged to question their clients' business.

A clerk handed Macdonnell his banknotes. Mac got up shakily and left the building.

The incident made the Americans even more aware that they were walking on a perilously narrow ledge between success and disaster. Despite all precautions, suspicion could easily be aroused through some chance over which they had no jurisdiction.

The knowledge that each day might be the last spent in freedom intensified their desire for self-indulgence. That evening after dinner Macdonnell and Noyes visited the Turkish Divan. Macdonnell was greeted enthusiastically by the management, and the three-piece orchestra brightened their tune as half a dozen couples moved on to the dance floor. February was the slackest month of the year for the entertainment business and the Divan was "dressed" with non-paying friends of the management and staff. Macdonnell's spirits began to lift as the floor manager led him up to his usual balcony table, at which he and Austin had spent many evenings during the last months.

Macdonnell sat down, nodding greetings to acquaintances. It was comforting to be recognized, to be admired. His pleasure increased as he noticed Frances Grey coming up the stairs to take their orders for drinks.

Pertly, the girl greeted the two Americans.

"Where's Dore?" she asked.

Theodore Bingham was the pseudonym that Austin had used to his mistress. Macdonnell fingered through his wallet. He pulled out £20 and a letter.

"These are from our poor friend," he said. "He is lying in a desperate condition."

In Macdonnell's eyes marriage numbered among the worst calamities.

"Whatever has happened?" Fanny Grey asked anxiously.

Sadly, Macdonnell shook his head.

"He has suffered a crippling shot-wound in the side," he said.

Fanny Grey tore open the letter and skimmed through it.

"But he says in the letter he's had a train crash," the girl objected. Macdonnell took a moment to absorb the complication.

"The ball was there before the accident, and it so affected him afterward that it had to be extracted," he decided. His expressive and experienced hands lifted the surgeon's knife, folded back the skin, tied off the arteries and extracted the shot.

"In fact I extracted the ball myself," he decided complacently.

There was a sharp noise. Noyes scraped his chair across the wooden floor. He found the conversation both frivolous and dull.

"So Theodore is indisposed," Fanny Grey ruminated. Macdonnell looked up sharply. There was an unmistakable invitation in her voice. Her wide-set green eyes swept appreciatively up his strong body, her mouth twisted into a mocking smile. Swiftly, he flung out his hand, clutching her thin wrist.

"If the master is abed the physician will take his place instead," he grinned.

Noyes found himself alone in the streets at 1 a.m. The air was crisp with the promise of snow as he walked slowly up the Haymarket where a few intrepid streetwalkers still lingered. It is hard to say why he chose Ellen Franklin. Perhaps, being a tender-hearted man, he was touched by her lack of overcoat on such a cold night. The girl accepted his agreement with surprise and delight. She clutched his arm, waved good night to her friends and tripped off with Noyes, chattering like a house sparrow.

Noyes woke up to a view of tiles and chimney-pots at No. 7 Charlotte Street, Rathbone Place. Two chairs, a wash-hand basin, and a table covered in faded baize completed the furnishings of Ellen Franklin's attic room. The girl had a fever. Noyes dressed and went out. He returned with a galvanic battery and a new pair of women's boots. He looked after Ellen all the weekend and decided to remain there indefinitely. Ellen introduced Noyes as her husband to the landlady and they moved into a spacious apartment on the drawing-room floor which they occupied at the cost of £5 10s. a week, including food.

The landlady found it strange that her prosperous new lodger had so few possessions, apart from a battery and a pair of woman's boots. Noyes had left his luggage at Durrant's Hotel until after he had bought a securely locking suitcase in which to hide his cash and private papers from the prying eyes of his mistress.

Ellen Franklin, a product of the slums, had a natural urge for self-preservation. She was merry, but avidly inquisitive; quick-witted but illiterate; always on the make but touching in her lack of expertise. Noyes armed himself against her chiseling questions with brief and inaccurate replies.

He told her that his name was Edwin Hall and that he had recently arrived from America. When she asked him why, he told her to mind her own business. When she persisted, he said he had come over to market a machine for milking cows. He admitted possessing sketches of this revolutionary instrument, but Ellen never found them. Their association was intimate physically, but mentally restrained.

George Bidwell continued to work the coup. He posted £4,642 in forged bills from Birmingham on February 8th. It was early on February 10th when he stormed into Macdonnell's rooms at the Grosvenor.

"Get up," he ordered. "Get up and start doing some work."

Macdonnell glared at the intruder. He sat up in his white silk nightshirt.

"But, my dear fellow, I yesterday supplied you with twelve magnificent forgeries all made out to leading discount houses," he protested.

George pulled a thick envelope from his pocket and threw it on to the bed.

"All these bills are not duplicates, but quadruplicates of bills I have already posted. You have repeated yourself again and again," he said disgustedly.

Macdonnell raised his eyebrows.

"But naturally," he said. "If the duplicates are acceptable to the Bank of England, what harm in repeating them?"

George extracted from the envelope two forgeries reproduced on the cheap blue paper used by the Rothschilds.

"Rothschilds have already been marked up as the acceptors of four forged bills amounting to £10,000. Austin told us that Rothschilds do not usually accept long paper. Supposing someone at the bank should be acquainted with this fact and grow suspicious of the amount of paper credited to their name?"

Macdonnell shrugged. He leaned over and poured himself a cup of tea from the tray on his bedside table. Bidwell continued lecturing.

"Suse and Sibeth, the London and Westminster Bank, the Anglo-Austrian Bank," he read through the acceptors of the other bills. "They have all been marked up for thousands of pounds already. I refuse to post any of them."

Macdonnell stared narrowly at George as he sipped his tea.

"I wish you to get up immediately and reproduce some bills of exchange on other discount houses," George said.

Macdonnell detested being pestered into action by anyone and Bidwell's approach was far from diplomatic. But he was nervous of George Bidwell's vicious tongue. Macdonnell had chosen to reproduce the simplest bills of exchange available. If he was now to branch into more complicated forgeries he must change his place of work.

"Without Austin to guard the door my room is continually invaded by chambermaids, valets and cleaners. I have no privacy," he grumbled petulantly.

"Well, go out and see what you can find," George snapped. He had no stomach for Macdonnell's procrastinations.

"I have been considering moving to a hotel owned, and consequently recommended, by my personal physician, Dr. Coulson," Macdonnell informed his chief crushingly. "It is situated in a *cul-de-sac* off St. James's."

"Very well." George pulled on his gloves and picked up his cane. "I will visit you there after dark this evening," he said.

Snow was dropping silently from an inky sky when George Bidwell strode down St. James's Street later that day. He turned left up St. James's Place, which opened into a small square surrounded by fine houses. This was a compact little residential area. Light shone dimly through the shuttered Georgian windows, but the basement kitchens were uncurtained, busy with cooks and scullery maids and noisy with preparations for the evening meal. George Bidwell turned north up the square, searching for Macdonnell's hotel. He glanced down a mews. Grooms rubbed down the steaming horses newly returned with their master's carriage from the City. A shaft of light blazed from a ground-floor window halfway up the square. George drew level with it and peered in. There was a large fire burning in the paneled room where a man was bending over a table in the middle of the room, unwrapping a machine of some kind. Bidwell froze. The man was Macdonnell, the machine a printing press. He lifted his cane, urgently rapping the window-pane.

Macdonnell leapt up and swung round to the window, shielding the machine with his body. But no uniformed policeman peered through the window and George had backed away. Macdonnell crossed swiftly to the window and rattled down the blinds. Bidwell smiled grimly from the shadows. He rang the bell of No. 17. A red-uniformed footman opened the door: he had pale blue eyes and a round, bucolic face.

"Is this an hotel?" George Bidwell asked him briskly.

"It is a private hotel reserved exclusively for officers and gentlemen," the footman replied.

"I wish to speak with a friend who arrived this afternoon," George said. Insolently, the footman looked Bidwell up and down.

"I will inform the Captain you are here," he said coldly. "What is the name?"

At that moment Macdonnell spoke to the footman from inside and Bidwell was admitted.

"My God, you gave me a shock by knocking on the window, Macdonnell complained as they entered his rooms.

"You must keep the blinds of the bedroom pulled down both night and day," George Bidwell warned him. They were standing in a small anteroom.

"My sitting-room," Macdonnell threw open the left-hand door. It was a charming room, paneled and green-painted, with Georgian furniture.

"Splendid fire," George said appreciatively.

"I have told the management I am newly arrived from South America and subject to chills." Macdonnell laughed.

Bidwell could only admire this choice of hideaway. No. 17 St. James's Place appeared a singularly unlikely establishment to harbor forgery on a grand scale, but in the event of surprise the square could be reached from the bedroom window, and the sitting-room window gave easy access to the mews.

Macdonnell turned up the gas burners and settled to work. Encouraged by the fact that the skilled committee of the Bank of England approved his workmanship, he quickly produced the last set of forgeries.

11

THE
LAST POSTING

Punctually at ten o'clock Edwin Noyes strode down the plush carpeted corridor of the London Bridge Terminus Hotel, glancing at the names of the residents written on slates outside each suite. He stopped at the one indicating Mr. Horton, unlocked the door and stepped inside. The room contained two brown leather upholstered chairs, a flat-topped desk possessing one drawer without a key, a waste-paper basket, pen, ink and paper renewable daily.

There was no one in the room, but a fire burned in the grate. Noyes unhinged his numbed fingers from the heavy black case he had been carrying, and crossed to the fire to warm his frozen hands. Despite the bitter morning, Noyes was humming happily to himself. Without a doubt he was already the best-paid clerk in the City and during the day he expected to earn a further £650 (£6,500 in terms of today's buying power). It was very satisfactory. Noyes turned from the fire, picked up his case and settled down to work at his desk with his notebooks piled around him.

It was February 14th, and the fraud machine had been purring along without a hitch for three weeks. The Americans had settled down to a routine. The day before, Noyes had shadowed George Bidwell to Birmingham for the fifth time. Nine forged bills, amounting to £14,686, had been posted to the Western Branch. A note was also enclosed to Colonel Francis, informing him that Mr. Warren was "gradually, but slowly, recovering from the fall from my horse and am succeeding thus far in matters of business to my wish." Mr. Warren had so far netted £45,000 and the scheme which started as a pinprick in the Bank of England's side was opening into a gaping wound.

But as money poured in, dispersal problems grew more acute and Noyes was hard put to it to keep the records accurate. He was checking the details of Mr. Warren's withdrawal book when there was a double knock on the door.

In a swift movement he swept the contents of his desk into the black case and clicked the lock shut before crossing to see who was there. A green-uniformed messenger was standing outside. He touched his peaked cap respectfully.

"Sorry, sir," he said, "but the bank refused to pay me."

Noyes stiffened. "Why?" he asked.

The grizzled face of the messenger looked blank.

"I couldn't say, sir. They seemed to be suspicious."

Suspicious? Noyes closed his eyes involuntarily as fear contracted the muscles of his stomach. He glanced furtively down the long passage, it was empty. With desperate eagerness he took the envelope the man held in his hand. It contained only the note which Noyes had given him to present at the Continental Bank.

Room No. 6, Terminus Hotel, London Bridge
Gentlemen. Please enclose amount in envelope.
E. Noyes for C.J.H.

An unpaid check for £65 fluttered softly to the ground. Quickly Noyes bent down and stuffed it into his pocket.

He pulled out some loose change, thanked the man briefly, and turned back into the room. Suddenly the strain of the last few weeks burst like a firework in his head. He began to panic. He cursed the familiar room for having no second exit and ran to the window. It was twelve feet from the ground. He peered through the white net curtains for any danger signal. Carriages and wagons trundled peacefully along the cobbled street. Watching the passers-by, he saw top-hats, bowlers and the round pillbox caps of messenger boys. There was not a policeman's helmet to be seen.

Noyes turned from the window, wiping his face with a nervous hand. He tried to tell himself there was nothing to worry about. It was just a small hitch which would be explained directly he reached the bank. He had taken the precaution of sending a decoy on ahead before withdrawing the sum of £14,686 from Bank of England funds. But the move had proved nothing. He would have to penetrate the bank in person to find out what was wrong.

Noyes seized his case and then realized he dare not take it with him. It was stuffed with clues connecting his name with Warren. All he required was Mr. Horton's check-book. He pulled it out, then looked through his wallet to be sure it still contained the agreement between himself and his fictitious employer. Grimly he set out for Lombard Street, shutting out the horrid thought that detectives might be waiting to apprehend him at the Continental Bank.

He discovered it was a false alarm. The manager had been concerned that the note had not been authentic. Noyes protested.

"I would be glad if you would obey instructions in my letters. Any messenger I send is necessarily trustworthy."

Fear gave authority to his words and Mr. Stanton was apologetic. Noyes accepted his regrets and went to the counter to cash one of Mr. Horton's checks for £6,000. Shaken, he walked out into the cold February sunshine. The incident was over, the manager's confidence in Mr. Horton remained unblemished, but Noyes was nervous. That day he scurried through his business, eager to get home. The next day it was worse. Everywhere he expected to be followed or accosted. He flinched when a stranger looked at him, jumped if he was pushed against or touched.

A project of such proportions brought tremendous mental pressures on the perpetrators. But if Macdonnell was feeling the strain he was not the man to show it. From the moment he stepped into the coffee-room of the Terminus Hotel on February 24th he was the focus of all eyes. It was useless for Bidwell to urge discretion, Macdonnell could never be anonymous. His vivid blue eyes and magnificent light brown beard were set off by the splendor of his clothes. His shirt was silk and monogrammed, his studs and cufflinks blazed with rubies. The Americans had decided to buy extravagantly and carry away as much wealth as they could on their backs. They were swamped with riches. Another huge sum of £14,686 had been posted in forged bills from Birmingham on February 20th.

Ingratiatingly, a waiter relieved Macdonnell of his cane, top-hat and gloves; another helped him off with his fur-lined overcoat.

"I will keep the case with me," Macdonnell said.

It was filled with banknotes recently changed for sovereigns at the Bank of England. Macdonnell strode across the thick carpet, between widely spaced tables, oblivious of the surreptitious stares of the tea-drinkers. He reached a corner table and sat down in a large armchair with a view of the entrance doors. The waiters exchanged anticipatory glances. Macdonnell had been a regular customer in the last weeks. They were convinced he was the Prince of Wales. The fact that he was invariably joined not by a beautiful socialite but by a simply-dressed City clerk intensified their curiosity. Five minutes later Macdonnell had finished his black coffee and was sipping a brandy as Noyes arrived from his office on the floor above. He was carrying his black case, which was identical to Macdonnell's and filled with sovereigns. One of the purposes of this regular meeting was to exchange cases.

Macdonnell smiled warmly at Noyes as he sat down at the table.

"Everything running along smoothly, dear fellow?" he asked lightly.

Noyes stared down at the white crocheted cloth.

"I find it all one hell of a strain," he muttered thickly.

Macdonnell's eyes widened. His remark had been purely conversational.

"I have carried four hundredweight of gold from the Bank of England, forty times I have visited the Continental Bank under threat of awkward questions or even sudden arrest, I have been buying U.S. bonds in thicker and thicker bundles," Noyes glared at Macdonnell, his voice edged with hysteria.

"Dear fellow, I will order you something immediately," Macdonnell lifted his right hand for service, the diamond rings glinting on three fingers. "Waiter, a double brandy for this gentleman." He turned and regarded his companion quizzically. "You are doing a splendid job," he said reassuringly. "No cause for anxiety at all."

Noyes blinked like a worried spaniel.

"I made an idiotic mistake the other day," he said hoarsely.

"And what might that have been?"

"I misspelled Horton 'Hoerton' when I endorsed a check of Warren's."

"Well?"

"The error was picked up by the Continental Bank and I resigned the check yesterday morning."

"In that case there is absolutely nothing to worry about," Macdonnell assured him. Noyes smiled wanly. Anxiety clouded his eyes again.

"Mac, would you do me a favor?"

"Why, certainly, old boy."

"I have a large case stuffed with bonds and valuables

back home. Would you take care of it for me? My mistress is a meddler, I do not trust her."

"Never fear, dear boy," Macdonnell said. "Immediately your glass is empty we will drive to your lodgings and remove the offending bag to my hotel."

In the cab Noyes explained briefly that on returning to his rooms from Westminster Abbey that morning he heard his mistress chattering in the basement where she was helping the landlady dish up the Sunday joint. He had taken the opportunity to unlock his private case and sort through the parcels of bonds and sovereigns, gold watches, jewelry and foreign currency. Suddenly he heard the door-latch click behind him and turned to find Ellen Franklin tiptoeing across the room.

"What's in that case, then?" she asked sharply.

"Mind your own business," he told her, slamming down the lid. But a packet of bonds was left on the floor.

Ellen reached them first.

"Hey, dearie, what are these?" she asked.

"Give them to me," Noyes ripped the packet from her hand. "Now get out," he ordered brutally.

Ellen had retired with a smirk, but Noyes was afraid he had roused her insatiable curiosity. And he was not wrong.

Ellen started to look for the key to the suitcase directly Noyes went out. Her search was rewarded when she tipped up a blue and gilt vase on the mantelshelf and the key fell out. In a moment she had unlocked the case, snatched out the packet and pulled ·the bonds from the envelope. She gave a pout of disgust. It was not the pile of banknotes she had imagined, but a roll of paper which she could not read. Ellen pushed them back into the envelope and ran off downstairs to consult her landlady. Mrs. White was excited with Ellen's discovery, but she could not read either.

"Here, Jesse," she called to her husband, "come and see what Ellen has found in her man's bag."

Mr. White was small and quiet-mannered. He came out of the pantry in his stockinged feet and took the packet from his wife's hand. He was a commission agent and recognized the U.S. bonds immediately. Thumbing through the bundle, which was thickly rolled, he noticed that each of the bonds was marked for $500 or $1,000. The packet was worth a small fortune.

"What shall I do with them, Mr. White?" Ellen asked breathlessly.

Mr. White looked at her mildly. His wife and the girl had grown highly suspicious of their quiet but prosperous lodger.

Mr. White sat down at the kitchen table and examined one of the bonds minutely. It appeared perfectly valid. He stared at the bundle. It was possible it was stolen property, but much more likely that the bonds were legitimate fees of a brilliant inventor.

"If I were you, my girl," he told Ellen severely, "I would put these back where they belong."

Ellen ran back upstairs, slipped the bonds into the case and relocked it. For some reason she did not unwrap the other parcels in the bag. Their contents would certainly have encouraged Mr. White to consult the police.

When Noyes and Macdonnell arrived at the house they went upstairs immediately. Ellen was sent out for some crystal cement to fasten the bonds, while Macdonnell addressed the envelope to Edward Noyes Hills, care of one of the leading hotels in New York. At the top left-hand corner of the envelope he wrote: "To await arrival."

"My God, I wish we were there now," Noyes said. "We each have a fortune already. Why do we go on?"

"I will register the packet for you tomorrow at the Royal Exchange Insurance Office," Macdonnell said mildly.

Secretly he agreed with Noyes. He was growing bored with the whole enterprise. He had ample cash for his

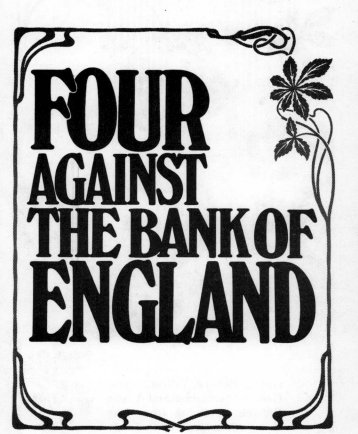

FOUR AGAINST THE BANK OF ENGLAND

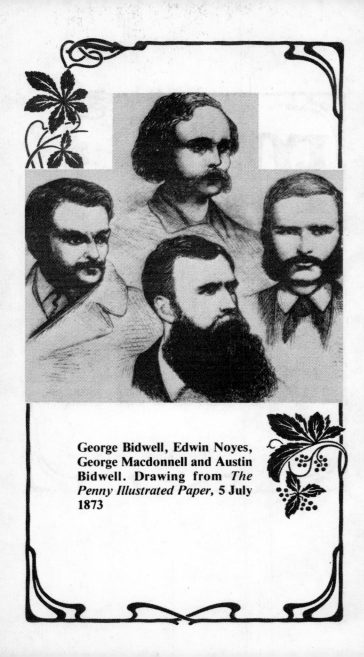

George Bidwell, Edwin Noyes, George Macdonnell and Austin Bidwell. Drawing from *The Penny Illustrated Paper,* **5 July 1873**

The facade of the Bank of England

35 Savile Row, corner-stone of
the conspiracy, before it was
demolished

Junction of Piccadilly and Regent Street

"Boys, that is the softest mark in the world." Under the top hats are Austin, Mac, and George. Illustration from *Forging His Own Chains*

The weighing-room of the Bank of England

Garraways coffee house where George and Macdonnell were celebrating when they heard of Noyes' arrest

St. James's Place—Macdonnell's hideaway was at No. 17

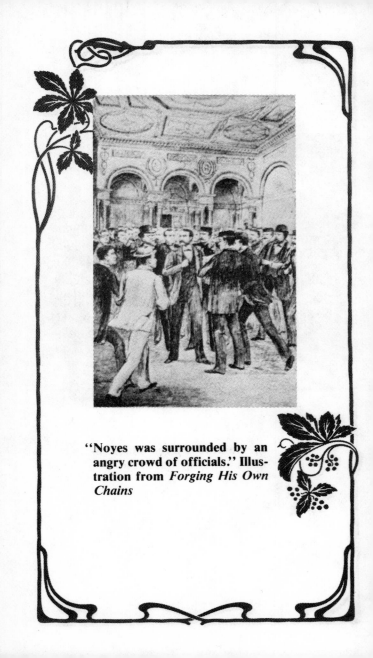

"Noyes was surrounded by an angry crowd of officials." Illustration from *Forging His Own Chains*

Duke's Road, Euston Square, where Nellie lived

Entrance to Euston Square Station, October 1870

The new hall, London and North Western Railway Station, Euston Square

George Bidwell

George Bidwell after his prison sentence. Frontispiece from *Forging His Own Chains*

BIDWELL'S TRAVELS.

FROM

Wall Street
To London Prison

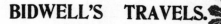

Fifteen Years in Solitude.

FREED A HUMAN WRECK, A WONDERFUL SURVIVAL AND A MORE
WONDERFUL RISE IN THE WORLD.
TO-DAY HE HAS A NATIONAL REPUTATION AS A WRITER, SPEAKER
AND IS CONSIDERED AN AUTHORITY ON ALL SOCIAL PROBLEMS.
HE WAS TRIED AT THE OLD BAILEY AND SENTENCED FOR LIFE,
CHARGED WITH THE £1,000,000 FORGERY ON THE BANK
OF ENGLAND.
THIS STORY SHOWS THAT THE EVENTS OF HIS LIFE SURPASS THE
IMAGINATIONS OF OUR FAMOUS NOVELISTS, ITS THRILLING
SCENES, HAIR-BREADTH ESCAPES AND MARVELOUS AD-
VENTURES ARE NOT A RECORD OF CRIME,
BUT ARE PROOFS OF THAT

IN THE WORLD OF WRONGDOING SUCCESS IS FAILURE.

490 Pages, 80 Graphic Illustrations.

Copyrighted 1897 by
BIDWELL PUBLISHING COMPANY,
HARTFORD, CONN,

The highly moral title page of
Forging His Own Chains

On trial at the Old Bailey, left to right: Austin, Macdonnell (leaning forward), George and Noyes

current requirements. He sealed the cement with his gold signet ring, which was engraved with the Macdonnell crest and motto *"Toujour Prest,"* or "Always ready," in antique French. He slipped the bonds into his pocket, picked up his friend's case and strolled out of the premises.

"Noyes is cracking," Macdonnell informed George Bidwell blithely when Bidwell called in as usual at St. James's Place the following morning.

"Cracking?"

Macdonnell told him the exact details.

It was due to George Bidwell's intricate and careful planning that the scheme had worked so far without a hitch. From the beginning he had adopted a highly professional attitude, studying each problem as it arose and acting promptly on his conclusions. This had engendered a feeling of confidence in Noyes and Macdonnell despite the risks they were running. Now, as he listened to Macdonnell, he sensed danger.

When Macdonnell had finished his explanation George Bidwell stared a moment at his nails before replying.

"I will dispatch the last batch of bills today," he said quietly. "Tell Noyes to be ready to leave the country by 1st March."

Macdonnell grinned.

"Excellent," he said. He cordially disliked Bidwell, but could only admire the man's decisiveness.

That Monday, February 24th, Bidwell dispatched the seventh and final installment of useless paper to the Western Branch. The packet was carefully registered and contained £19,000 in forged bills. The Bank of England swallowed another sugar-coated pill without protest.

George Bidwell had achieved his object, the last batch of forged bills were in the post. The whole project had been fantastically successful and now they were free to collect the remainder of their fortune and disappear.

But February is a short month and the three men were faced with the formidable task of disposing of £19,000 in four days. The pace quickened to a scramble as Noyes withdrew the cash in checks for U.S. bonds and banknotes and changed them into sovereigns. Macdonnell raced about the City changing the sovereigns back again to banknotes and with them buying other bonds. To relieve the congestion in their suitcases many of the bonds were parceled up, registered, and posted to the States to await their arrival at various hotels and safe deposits in New York.

George Bidwell was left free to consider the plans for departure. He decided to clear Paternoster Row immediately of all incriminating material. George had always paid cash for blocks and stamps when he took delivery of them, but now he visited each firm to check every order he had given during the previous two months. He assured himself that each sketch he had supplied had been returned, and every other scrap of paper connected with these orders was either thrown away or given back to him.

George ran up against a snag at Thomas Straker's when he was informed that one of his orders had been printed by lithography. The text was embedded in a huge stone which would be inconvenient to carry away.

"Can I see it?" George asked.

"Why certainly, sir. Delighted," said Mr. Straker.

He was proud of his little firm and an excellent craftsman who never tired of explaining the wonders of engraving techniques. Talking continuously, he conveyed George through the outer office into the printing-room. Under the curious eyes of several workmen and apprentices George examined the huge limestone on the lithographic press. Before him lay the perfect passport to disaster. It was a beautifully executed original lithograph of a forged bill on the London and Westminster Bank which George had posted the day before to Colonel Francis.

Bidwell's eyes narrowed. He smothered an urge to strike the stone with his cane.

"Is it possible to erase these impressions?" he asked.

"Why, yes, of course. We can use these stones again and again. There are some wonderful new developments connected with this type of printing . . ."

"How?"

"How? Oh, yes, how are these impressions erased? We do it with Water of Ayr or snake stone."

"Will you show me how it's done?" George could not hide his eagerness.

"Why, yes," said Mr. Straker happily. A few minutes later he looked up.

"If you offered me a hundred pounds, Mr. Brooks, I could not produce another bill from that stone without re-transferring it."

Bidwell peered down at the blank surface.

"Very good," he said.

He turned and hurried back through the outer office and into the street. Now that every priority was being given to unobtrusive departure, the question of what to do with the two women became of paramount importance. If they were deserted at this stage there was no telling what harm they might do out of revenge.

"We must take them with us," George declared.

But Noyes, for once, protested.

"You do what you like, George," he said, "but I'm certainly not taking Ellen."

The girl was a menace and Noyes had grown exasperated with her.

"It's up to you," George told him. "If you can get away without suspicion."

Noyes thought that he could. Now the first excitement had worn off, his mistress was growing increasingly restive. Having failed to build Noyes into a criminal she had become bored with him. Noyes was sure she could be safely paid off, providing the farewell present was substantial.

Nellie Vernon and Frances Grey, on the other hand, had been intimates of the Americans for many months and might reasonably have suspicions to air abroad when they read details of the forgeries. It was therefore decided to take Nellie and Fanny to the States while Ellen Franklin would be left behind.

Fanny accepted Macdonnell's offer to take her with him to America providing her girl friend could accompany them.

George Bidwell's mistress was in a hip bath in front of the drawing-room fire when she heard the news.

"Our troubles are over, Nellie," he told her briskly. "We sail for the States in four days' time."

Nellie blinked through the steam at George.

"America?" she queried.

Her brown eyes shone with astonishment, her hair hung in damp coils round her childish face. George felt passion surging through his veins. He tore off his scarf and overcoat.

"Time to get out of the bath," he urged.

Obediently, Nellie stood up, the water poured from her lean, boyish body, the skin of her breasts shone with moisture.

"My towel, quick, quick, my towel, George. It is warming by the fire."

Bidwell picked up the towel and wrapped it swiftly round her. His lips crushed the skin at the nape of her neck. Nellie half-turned her head toward him.

"Your wife?" she asked urgently. "What about your wife?"

George could not think of an answer. And then he remembered the necklace. He fumbled in his pocket and pulled out a long string of diamonds.

"For you," he said, his cold eyes glinting.

He clipped them round her naked throat, lifted the girl in his arms and carried her through to bed.

Bidwell nudged Nellie awake at 6 a.m. next morning.

"Time to get up and pack. We leave at noon," he told her.

Nellie groaned.

"Today?" she murmured. "I thought it was four days."

"We are moving to the Albemarle Hotel for a couple of nights before we sail," he said, bending to fix his sock suspender. "You will tell them there we have just arrived from Paris."

At noon, as the luggage was being carried to a cab, Macdonnell called in to report progress; then a salesman arrived with a bag for George and had to be paid off. Consequently, one or two items were overlooked and later found by Mrs. Grove when she cleaned the room. Four bill forms remained at the back of a drawer and a photographic lens had slipped behind the looking glass. They were kept carefully in case the Bidwells returned for them.

It was late on Tuesday evening, February 25th, when Noyes called at the Albemarle Hotel. He informed George Bidwell that the dispersal operation was virtually complete. In three hectic days he had drained Mr. Warren's account of all but a few hundred pounds. Bidwell congratulated him. The Bank of England was still sleeping soundly. It was time to slip quietly away.

12

HUNDRED-THOUSAND-POUND
ERROR

On Wednesday, February 26th, the three men dissolved their highly rewarding partnership at a farewell luncheon at one of London's most exclusive restaurants. Afterward they stepped out into Piccadilly. Icy rain spat viciously in their faces, a cruel wind twisted their overcoats around their knees, a passing carriage hurled mud over their fine new leather boots. But even the miseries of the fag-end of an English winter receded before the Americans' irrepressible high spirits as they battled through to St. James's Place.

Macdonnell locked the door of his rooms and put some more coal on the fire. His friends drew up their chairs.

"We commit to the flames all clues connecting ourselves with the greatest fraud in history," Macdonnell proclaimed.

George pulled from his trouser pocket two black notebooks. He threw them on to the blaze.

"A meticulous record of our accounts," he said.

Noyes ferreted in his case and withdrew two of Mr. Warren's check-books, a wad of Horton's credit slips and a stack of receipts for bonds and securities. He dropped them thankfully into the fire.

"Burn, burn, the fire will lick us clean," Macdonnell crowed, pulling forward Bidwell's old tin trunk. He stoked up the flames with colored paper, printers' proofs, wood engraving blocks and unused bill forms.

At last the trunk was empty. All was destroyed except

the pile of discarded forgeries which Macdonnell had kept ceremoniously for the final conflagration.

He sat back in his chair, thumbing lovingly through the bundle, which represented hours of intricate workmanship.

"Perfect works of art," he murmured sadly. "Shame! Shame! To destroy them all."

Bidwell regarded the bundle casually.

"Are they good enough to send in, Mac?"

"We have only the details to fill in," he answered.

"Then get down and fill them in," Bidwell's voice cracked out into the warm and peaceful room. Swiftly, Macdonnell rose and moved over to the desk. In a few minutes he had filled in the final details of twenty-four forged bills while Bidwell watched with greedy eyes.

Throwing caution to the winds, the three men traveled up to Birmingham the following day and posted these bills to Colonel Francis. They had hoisted the total sum of the forgeries to the total of £100,000, the equivalent of a million pounds today. But the capacity to know when to stop is a vital requirement of all gamblers. George Bidwell and his accomplices had gone too far.

The packet of forgeries was lying snugly on Colonel Francis' massive, green-leather-topped desk on Friday, February 28th. Punctually at 10 a.m., Colonel Francis walked down the great curved Adam staircase, from his apartments above, into the pillared banking hall. A liveried footman unbolted and swung open the huge main doors and the cashier moved to the counters to serve the first customers hurrying in from the street. The Colonel nodded urbanely to a prosperous client and turned into his office. He opened his mail with an ivory knife and passed the items to be checked into his out-tray. Among them the contents of the registered packet from Birmingham addressed in the now familiar handwriting of Mr. Warren.

Later in the morning the discount clerk, checking

through Mr. Warren's bills in the ordinary course of duty, had cause to consult the manager.

"Excuse me, sir," he apologized as he stepped into the Colonel's room, "but I think I should draw your attention to these."

He handed the Colonel two of Mr. Warren's bills of exchange for £1,000 each.

"The dates of issue seem to be missing."

"Quite correct," agreed the Colonel, more pleased with his employee's efficiency than troubled by any discrepancy in the bills. "It must be an oversight on the part of the acceptors."

He glanced at the acceptor's name. It was B. W. Blydenstein & Co. of 20 Great St. Helens, a banking house of impeccable reputation.

"Send them down to Blydenstein's for correction," the Colonel instructed. "There is no hurry, the messenger can deliver them on his normal rounds this afternoon."

So it was that an anonymous bank messenger precipitated one of the most embarrassing revelations the Bank of England has ever known. For Blydenstein's could find no trace of the bills in their issue books. The apalling news reached Colonel Francis in a letter from Blydenstein's marked "Urgent and Confidential." Tearing open the envelope, the Colonel read the terse sentence, "We have no record of these bills and can only assume they are forgeries." Signed, "William Henry Trumpler Member."

Forgeries! This dreadful word, almost foreign to the banking vocabulary of Colonel Francis, threw him into a state of extreme agitation. He rang for Mr. Warren's file. The last entry was a memorandum from the discount clerk stating that £24,265 had been discounted to Mr. Warren that day on bills of exchange received. A small gasp of horror escaped the Colonel as he read the name of Rothschild listed twice among the acceptors of the bills. Had he passed through forged bills on the name of one of the directors of the Bank of England?

The Colonel grabbed his hat and overcoat and, stuffing Mr. Warren's file into his briefcase, rushed out to find a hansom cab. The streets were clogged with homeward-bound office workers, on foot or in horse buses, and it took well over thirty minutes to reach Threadneedle Street, where he at once sought out Mr. May, Deputy Chief Cashier of the Bank of England.

The practiced eye of Mr. May immediately noticed some strange irregularities in Mr. Warren's file. The customer was singularly lacking in credentials. There were no permanent address, no references, no introduction by a director, only large and frequent disbursements made to a Mr. Horton and passed through the Continental Bank in Lombard Street.

"Appalling," Mr. May muttered as he read. "The Bank of England duped by one of her own customers. It is unthinkable."

He looked sharply across at Colonel Francis.

"Am I to understand the perpetrator of this outrage is a foreigner—an American?" he asked. The Colonel admitted that he was.

"Disgusting."

For an Englishman to rob the Bank of England was comparable to picking the pocket of one's grandmother but for a foreigner to do so was an outrage.

"I cannot imagine what the directors will say to all this," sighed Mr. May. He looked at his watch. It was now too late to make inquiries in the City, the matter would have to wait until the morning. He dismissed the Colonel with a grim "Good night."

The fascinating question which remained was whether the forgers would get away before the bank completed its inquiries and the ponderous machine of justice could be cranked into action. It was already the last day of February and George and his companions were due to sail immediately.

The forgers spent a thoroughly successful Friday making the final clearances and Noyes withdrew £28,500 from Horton's account. That evening George cabled Austin in Havana: "All is safely gathered in."

Unfortunately, this was not an exact statement. Noyes had one more call to make. On Saturday morning, March 1st, he was one of the first customers to be served at the Continental Bank. He had come to clear the Horton account of a final £8,000. He asked for a mixture of English and foreign money and was requested to call back for the foreign exchange later in the morning.

Leaving the bank, Noyes walked happily round to Garraway's coffee house in Exchange Alley where his companions were celebrating with almost hysterical delight the culmination of their dreams.

That Saturday morning the usually serene atmosphere in the marble halls of the Bank of England was exploded by the wildest rumors. The Deputy Chief Cashier had cancelled his engagements and was abroad early in the City making urgent inquiries. He visited Blydenstein's, Rothschild's and the Continental Bank, whose revelations only confirmed his worst fears.

His final call was to Messrs. Freshfields, Solicitors to the Bank of England. Here Mr. May was able to mitigate his terrible news with the hope that Mr. Horton, as well as Mr. Warren, would be in custody by lunchtime.

Mr. May arranged for the plain-clothes detective, who was always on duty at the Bank of England, to follow Mr. Horton's clerk out of the Continental Bank at noon to his final hideout and accomplices.

But here fate stepped in to save the forgers. When a messenger informed May that Horton's clerk had arrived at the Continental Bank he immediately sent for the detective. But by some mischance the man could not be found and May was forced to leave without him.

Bank employees were amazed to see the dignified

figure of the Deputy Chief Cashier sprinting through the marble corridors, across the main hall, and out into Threadneedle Street. He was engulfed in the seething traffic of the cross-roads, only to reappear momentarily before diving down Lombard Street. Here the breathless Mr. May saw Police Constable No. 622 marching slowly along on his beat. Dashing over, he clutched him by the arm, gasped out, "I have someone for you to take into custody," and propelled him through the side entrance of the Continental Bank.

Noyes had arrived at the Continental Bank to collect his foreign currency and was asked to wait until it was counted through. He was sitting in a corner chair when he heard a commotion on the other side of the counter. The next moment a small posse of men in coat-tails exploded into the main banking hall. Noyes' original surprise curdled to terror as he realized that he was the focus of their eyes. As he rose, the foremost man shouted at him.

"Are you Mr. Horton's clerk?"

"I am," he replied.

"This is your man, Constable." Mr. May stood aside and waved Constable Jonathan Pope forward. At the sight of the policeman the whole banking hall burst into an uproar.

"Why are you giving me into custody?" Noyes demanded furiously.

"I am from the Bank of England and challenge you with fraud," answered Mr. May.

Fraud against the Bank of England! The words spread from mouth to mouth through the City streets.

Waiting in Garraways, George and Macdonnell had begun to wonder why Noyes was delayed when they heard the first whisper of fraud, and immediately rushed out into Lombard Street in search of their friend.

A bulging, heaving mass of humanity had oozed out of the Continental Bank and was moving slowly but irrevocably toward Bow Lane Police Station. George and Macdonnell ran toward the crowd and elbowed their way between the frock-coated businessmen until they discovered Noyes and his escort. Noyes was protesting vehemently amidst the general hubbub.

"I don't know what all this is about . . . it is intolerable to be treated in this way . . . I am only Mr. Horton's clerk," when he suddenly saw George. No sign of recognition escaped him, but he stopped in his tracks and shouted:

"I wish to be taken straight to Mr. Horton."

The policeman hesitated.

"Where is Mr. Horton's office?" he asked.

"At the Terminus Hotel," Noyes replied.

But the policeman refused to be led astray.

"I must take you to the station first," he said. "We will get in touch with Mr. Horton from there."

George and Macdonnell eased out of the crowd of inquisitive Londoners and slipped down a side-street.

"My God, George, what do we do now?"

"Do?" replied George. "We do nothing. Ed has a perfect alibi. I expect him to be freed in forty-eight hours."

"But what about us?"

"A small alteration in our plans. Departure postponed. There is no shred of evidence to connect our names with the crime."

George hailed a passing hansom.

"I am returning home to lunch," he said. "Please collect Ed's luggage from his lodgings, he has £3,000 in U.S. bonds there. I will contact you late at St. James's Place."

13

HIDE-AND-SEEK
GAME

It soon became clear to the City Police that this was no ordinary case of larceny when P. C. Jonathan Pope arrived back at Bow Lane Police Station with Noyes in charge. The prisoner was questioned, searched, photographed and taken down to a cell. Then the Commissioner arrived in a state of cold-eyed determination to take charge of investigations, officers were sent to check the truth of Noyes' verbal statement, while others supervised the stream of visitors to his cell.

The reports which filtered back to the station were disappointing. Mr. Horton was not in his office when the police called and a search of the room revealed nothing. No luggage was found at Durrant's Hotel, which Noyes had given as his address. Messrs. Kino of 46 Lombard Street had no record of making a suit for Noyes, although his coat carried their label.

When Colonel Francis visited the cells he had to admit that he had never set eyes on Noyes before and none of the cashiers of the Western Branch recognized him either.

A special sitting of the Justices was held at the Mansion House at 2 p.m. that afternoon. The usual business of the day had ended at noon. The Justice room was almost empty except for court officials and several newspaper reporters when Noyes was led to the bar. The correspondent of the *Echo* had barely time to sketch in the prisoner's characteristics—"a well-dressed young man of gentlemanly appearance and manners"—when the Lord Mayor took his seat on the bench and ordered the court to be cleared. He was taking the unprecedented step of conducting the hearing *in camera*. Messers. Freshfields, Solicitors of the Bank of England, were able to persuade the Lord Mayor, Sir Sydney Waterlow, to remand Noyes in custody for a week. Noyes was not represented by counsel.

Immediately the proceedings were over, a notice was issued by the City police office and widely circulated, offering £500 reward for the apprehension of "F. A. Warren, alias C. J. Horton." There followed a description of the wanted man, pieced together by the staff of the Western Branch.

> About forty years of age. 5 ft. 9 in. or 10 in. in height. Thin, dark, sallow, with dark hair and eyes, speaking with a strong American accent and dressed fairly well in a frock-coat and loose brown overcoat.

Although accurate in most particulars, this was hardly a flattering portrait of the elegant, thirty-year-old Austin Bidwell.

The size of the reward offered was directly attributable to the outrage of the directors of the Bank of England. The bank had suffered many crises in 180 years, but it had never been so drastically swindled. To add to the humiliation, the forgers had eluded capture because of the laxity of a detective at the Bank of England. Now, with the criminals at large, it was impossible to keep the matter hushed up. The Press would pounce upon the news and glaringly expose the violation of the impregnable Bank of England. The directors were prepared to stop at nothing, whatever the cost, to vindicate the bank's reputation and bring the forgers to justice.

Meanwhile George Bidwell had calmly enjoyed a pleasant and unhurried lunch with his mistress in the

Albemarle Hotel dining-room. George Macdonnell's attitude was more realistic. Normally light-hearted and inconsequential, nevertheless he did not delude himself and was seized with terrible anxiety. The prospect of visiting the arrested man's lodgings filled him with the utmost apprehension but twenty minutes after the arrest he was hammering on the door of No. 7 Charlotte Street.

Ellen Franklin poked her head round the door, and Macdonnell pushed his way unceremoniously into the house.

"I have some very bad news for you, Ellen," he said. "Come on upstairs."

In Noyes' rooms he looked round for the luggage and dragged two trunks from under the bed. He tried to open the large one. It was locked, but the other was empty. In frantic haste he began to throw all Noyes' belongings into it. Ellen pursued him from wardrobe to closet, chattering with alarm.

On the way upstairs Macdonnell had decided not to tell the girl the truth and parried her string of questions with vague replies. Ed had to catch a train in a hurry, he had been called away unexpectedly, he had not mentioned where he was going. Thud. A pair of boots landed heavily in the trunk and a bulky envelope slid out of one leg. It was the bonds. Macdonnell dived forward and slipped the envelope into his pocket. The packing nearly over, he turned to Ellen Franklin.

"Look, here is £20 to tide you over," he said. "I will call by in a few days to make sure you are well. Now just finish off that trunk for me."

Ellen knelt down and crammed the remaining oddments down the sides of the case. She was highly suspicious and frightened by this unexpected change.

"I can't understand it. It's not like Ed to go away without saying goodbye."

"He'll be back in no time," Macdonnell reassured

her, and dashed off downstairs to get the cab-driver to carry down the trunks.

On the bend of the stairs he froze. A man in a dark mackintosh was standing in the doorway talking to the landlord.

Macdonnell fled upstairs again.

"Who is that in the hall?" he asked Ellen.

"Goodness, I cannot tell you," she answered.

"Then go and find out," he commanded.

He had fortunately overestimated the speed of police inquiries. The caller was only a man in search of lodgings. Noticing Macdonnell's ashen face and obvious alarm, Ellen grew hysterical. She refused to let him take the luggage away, insisting it was perfectly safe with her until Ed returned. In the end she allowed Macdonnell to take one of the trunks, but he had to leave the other behind. Ellen tried unsuccessfully to hear the directions Macdonnell gave the driver, but persuaded the landlord to note down the number of the cab before it disappeared round the corner of the street.

Macdonnell was driven straight to St. James's Place. And now even the secure familiarity of his own rooms dissolved before his suspicious eyes. He pulled up the blinds for the first time in weeks; watery daylight revealed a ceiling blackened by smoke and burners cracked from the continual pressure of the gas. A picture hung askew; its glass had been used by Macdonnell for his forging. There were numerous pots of ink on the writing desk which was badly burned by cigarette ends. To a practiced eye these vital trivial details would present an overall picture of a forger's workshop.

Macdonnell was surrounded by half-filled trunks when George walked in, shutting the door carefully behind him.

"I forbid you to leave," he said quietly.

Macdonnell lost his temper.

"It is a fantastic and deluded policy to do nothing," he spluttered. "We have a head start, we must get away while there is still time to leave the country unchallenged. It is lunacy to remain."

But George utterly refused to budge.

The key to this unrealistic decision lay in the extremes of George's character. His stubbornness and pride had been fortified by the successes of the last few months. Now he refused to admit that anything serious had gone wrong, yet at the same time felt compelled, from paternal motives, to remain in England until Noyes was released. His final argument was that it would create unnecessary suspicion for an American to leave his lodgings precipitously. The outcome of the altercation was inevitable. George remained adamant, while Macdonnell cooled down and apologized.

In contrast to the dramatic happenings of the previous day, Sunday, March 2nd, passed without incident. For Macdonnell the lack of action was scarcely endurable. As the day dragged on he decided three times to leave his lodgings and three times changed his mind.

By Monday morning fifty-six precious hours had slipped away since Noyes had been arrested, and the hotel staff were beginning to murmur over the eccentricities of Captain Macdonnell. At breakfast guests peered round their papers in surprise when the tomblike silence of the room was broken by Macdonnell's loud complaints. The eggs were overcooked, the coffee tasted vile and he demanded to see every morning paper that was published. Perusal of these newspapers only intensified his anxiety.

"GREAT FORGERIES IN THE CITY," *The Times* proclaimed in bold capitals upon its leader page:

It was discovered on Saturday that bills to an enormous amount had been forged upon all the principal houses in the City of London and that these bills had been discounted by the Bank of England. Notice was therefore given to bankers, brokers and others not to accept, receive or negotiate any of the undermentioned securities of the United States.

There followed a list of numbers of U.S. bonds stretching to forty-five lines of type, a description of Mr. Warren, details of the proffered reward and a report of the Mansion House proceedings. The final paragraph ran:

The forged bills are said to have been admirably executed, the signatures, the print, the paper, the stamps, etc., having been so carefully counterfeited as almost to defy detection.

The story was repeated in the *Echo,* the *Daily Telegraph,* the *Standard* and the *City Press*. The *New York Times* reported a cable from London telling of frauds on the Bank of England "on a gigantic scale," and continued:

They have been committed by one Warren, alias Horton, an American, through skillful forgeries of the names of the Rothschilds and other great financial houses. A reward of $1,000 is being offered for him. The police are searching.

Macdonnell scraped back his chair and strode out to the manager's office.

"May I have my bill, please. I think I will leave today, I have some business to do in Paris," he told Mr. Herold, the manager.

"Will you not wait?" he replied. "It is such bad weather for traveling."

Macdonnell paused.

"Yes, I will wait. I will not go," he said.

He was dizzy with nerves and indecision. After a further two hours' exhausting heart-searching he paid the bill at one o'clock and asked for a cab immediately.

"Shall I forward your mail to you, Captain?" asked Mr. Herold.

"Oh, no," Mac answered. "I am only going to Paris, I will be back tonight."

This unlikely statement hardly lulled the manager's growing suspicions.

"You are a very quick traveler," he remarked.

When the cab arrived Mac refused to allow his luggage to be strapped on the roof because of the pelting rain. It was piled inside the cab. Another cab was called and when the last hat-box had been squeezed in there was no room for the passenger.

"What an extraordinary man," commented the manager as Macdonnell, in top-hat and immaculate overcoat, stepped out into the deluge of rain and escorted the two cabs into St. James's.

Meanwhile police had been scouring London for clues to the whereabouts of Mr. Warren. The Golden Cross Hotel was listed in the Bank of England file as Mr. Warren's address. On Monday morning two detectives inquired for him there. The receptionist regretted that Mr. Warren's room had been canceled two days ago. The detectives showed their badges and asked to see the manager. Every porter, waiter and chambermaid was interviewed that morning and not one of them had the slightest recollection of Mr. Warren. He had paid for his room for eleven months, but had not slept in the bed for a single night.

Mr. Green, the Savile Row tailor, had a different address for Mr. Warren. It was 21 Enfield Road, Haggerstone. The landlady at this address had never heard of Mr. Warren. But she remembered a charming American who had admired her cooking excessively. She found a letter from him in her writing-case and the police took it away.

Mr. Warren's only other known address was the Post Office, Birmingham. But inquiries there revealed that Mr. Warren's mail had invariably been collected by a cab-driver.

The questioning of Noyes was renewed. He refused to say where he had lodged since he left Durrant's Hotel. Protesting that he was an innocent clerk, he referred to the *Daily Telegraph* advertisement and his employment agreement with Mr. Horton, which had been found in his wallet when he was arrested. He continually reiterated that if his master indulged in criminal activities he was completely ignorant of them.

Police methods might be slow and cumbersome but there was a relentless persistence about them. Detectives once again visited the Lombard Street tailor whose name tab was sewn into Noyes' suit. Each salesman was sent to Bow Lane to see Noyes in his cell. Not one of them recognized him. Just as the detectives were leaving the tailor's premises the manager asked if inquiries had been made at their Regent Street branch. The detectives moved on to 87 Regent Street. The stock-room was placed at their disposal and here, among the shelves stacked with bolts of gentlemen's suiting, they interrogated every member of the staff.

Henry Thomas Hagger, one of the salesmen, recognized the photograph which the police showed him. It was a regular customer of his named Brooks. Mr. Brooks always collected his clothes in person and paid for them immediately. He had not been introduced by anyone, but had just walked into the shop alone. He had always been alone.

Hagger fetched his order book and checked through Mr. Brooks' orders. There were three, and at the bottom of the second was an address: Nelson's Hotel, Great Portland Street.

It was at Nelson's Hotel that the police first heard of Noyes' friends and compatriots, the Bidwells and George Macdonnell. All these men had used the hotel as a base address for their U.S. mail. But the significance of this discovery was lost on the detectives. The names they desperately hoped, but failed, to find in the hotel register were C. J. Horton and F. A. Warren.

Newspaper reports of the fraud had aroused such public outcry that every American visitor to London was being viewed with suspicion. Police headquarters at Old Jewry were deluged with supposedly vital information about the forgers.

When this was sorted through on Wednesday morning by the chief detectives working on the case their attention was riveted by a report on the suspicious behavior of a certain Captain Macdonnell. Sergeant Smith was dispatched to St. James's Place to follow up the excited surmise of Miss Green and her manager, Franz Joseph Herold.

Sergeant Smith discovered he had missed Macdonnell by some hours and nothing appeared to be left behind except a classified City directory. He searched the rooms meticulously and when he raked out the ashes of the fireplace he found four torn-up balls of blotting paper which had not been completely burned. The Sergeant carried his finds into the hotel kitchen and ironed them flat. When he had pieced the charred remains together he was able to decipher such parts of phrases as "acceptable payable at," "The Bank of Belgium and Holland," "ten thousand" and other words and signatures which clearly indicated a connection with the forgeries. Soon after the jubilant Sergeant returned to headquarters a notice was pinned to the police board. It offered £500 for the capture of George Macdonnell.

The classified directory which was found in Macdonnell's rooms subsequently provided a useful clue. The pages listing wood and metal engravers were missing and there were ticks against the names of printers used by the forgers.

By Wednesday, March 5th, five days after the fraud had been discovered, George Bidwell was still clinging to the fatal idea that his safety was not in jeopardy. He

had taken Nellie to the seaside for a few days, where
they stayed at the Victoria Hotel, St. Leonards, under
the name of Bidwell. It was incredible that at a time
when the whole country was ringing with news of the
forgeries the leader of the conspirators was staying under his own name at one of the most frequented hotels
in the land, courting detection every hour of the day.

George had read the newspaper reports with relish.
The only item which afforded him some aggravation
was the mention that Noyes had not been represented
by counsel at the magistrates' hearing. He repaired the
omission early on Wednesday morning by driving over
to Dover and dispatching a draft for £300 to David
Howell, the Cheapside solicitor who had drawn up
Noyes' contract with Horton. He instructed Howell to
undertake Noyes' defense.

At that moment George Bidwell could have boarded
the cross-channel steamer and been safely on the Continent by nightfall. Instead this extraordinary man
caught the first train in the opposite direction. As the
steady rhythm of the wheels carried him back to London, George read the morning papers.

For the third day running the national dailies each
filled an entire column with comment, rumor and surmise about the forgeries, for, as the *Daily Telegraph*
complained petulantly: "Those in possession of the
facts decline to make them public." The editorials
unanimously praised the amazing ingenuity of the plot
and audacity of the forgers.

George Bidwell suddenly became uneasy. He had
read for the first time that it was not mischance but a
gross error which had led to discovery of the forgeries.
Macdonnell had always been unpredictable, but it was
indeed astonishing that George Bidwell himself had not
noticed the mistake. Conscious that the smallest slip
might prove fatal, it had invariably been his practice
to check through all the forged bills before he posted

them. The revelation of his fallibility gave a nightmare quality to the long months of meticulous attention to detail.

But worse was to follow. Macdonnell did not keep his appointment with George at the Grosvenor Hotel that morning. Bidwell then drove down to 80 Tachbrook Street, where Macdonnell was living with Frances Grey, but he was not there either. Fanny told George that a stranger had called at the house asking for Captain Macdonnell. As it was unthinkable that Macdonnell would have given his address to a stranger at this critical time, George was forced to the conclusion that the caller had been a detective already on Macdonnell's trail.

George Bidwell realized he had finally underestimated the British police. For the first time he faced his predicament. He was a wanted man and a continent away from home.

But Macdonnell had not been apprehended. When he arrived back at Tachbrook Street early that afternoon after George had left, no detective stepped forward to arrest him, although he had been traced to that address.

With admirable alacrity the City police had traced Captain Macdonnell from St. James's Place to the Turkish Divan and from there to his mistress's lodgings. Sergeant Bull had gone immediately to 80 Tachbrook Street with a warrant for Macdonnell's arrest. As Macdonnell was not there, the Sergeant returned to headquarters. If watch had been kept on the house for only a few hours both Macdonnell and George Bidwell might have been taken.

When Macdonnell heard about his visitor he realized that the police were on his heels. Since he had bolted from St. James's Place he had been quivering with impatience to leave England, and now he drove to the shipping offices and inquired about the next boat to New York. He booked three passages on the *Peruvian,* sailing from Liverpool the next day, and sent off his luggage by rail in the name of Grey.

But there was one trunk which required special treatment. He dashed down to Moorgate Street and arranged for the North Atlantic Shipping Company to dispatch the trunk direct to New York. It was labeled:

Major Geo. Matthews,
c/o Atlantic Express Co.
57 Broadway, New York
Contents: Wearing apparel actually in use.
TO BE KEPT IN BOND UNTIL CALLED FOR
Sender: Charles Lessing, Tunbridge Wells, Kent.

Between the layers of soiled clothes were neatly folded some $225,000 worth of U.S. bonds.

Macdonnell dared not return to Tachbrook Street, but telegraphed his mistress to meet him at Gatti's in Lowther Arcade. Here he slipped two tickets for the boat into her hand, and told her to catch the 9:15 p.m. train to Liverpool and to wait for him at the North Western Station Hotel. Fanny did as she was told, but she and her companion waited in vain for him to join them at the hotel.

For directly Macdonnell reached Liverpool he realized he was being followed. He doubled back on to the platform and leapt on to a moving train. When the train arrived at Chester some hours later he changed again. For Taunton. He eventually reached Southampton by a highly unorthodox route by noon next day, but had thrown off his pursuers. He bought a ticket on the cross-channel packet to Le Havre and only felt safe when he reached his beloved Paris.

Macdonnell was a man with a long list of aliases, but for some astonishing reason he used his own name when he booked into the Hôtel Richmond, Rue du Helder, in Paris. Again under his own name he bought a ticket for the S.S. *Thuringia* leaving for New York on March 8th.

Sailing out into the Atlantic, one week after the discovery of the forgeries, Macdonnell left in his wake a trail of clues as flagrantly obvious as pieces in a paper chase.

14

LOSING
CAT LIVES

The events of the next twelve hours were extraordinary. George Bidwell was fully aware that the police trap was closing yet he still lingered in London, frittering away the precious hours on a string of comparatively unimportant details.

On Thursday morning, March 6, he still had the edge on the police. They were looking not for him but for Frederick Albert Warren. The City police were convinced that Warren was still at large in the metropolis, and to prevent him slipping quietly out of town a watch was kept on all the main railway termini from dawn on Thursday.

Sergeant William Smith stamped his feet and flexed his hands inside his black leather gloves. It was a bone-chilling morning and his two-hour vigil at Charing Cross had yielded nothing. Early trains had disgorged an army of frock-coated office workers, and now wheezed softly beside the ticket barriers, their smoke curling lazily upward toward the high steel girders of the roof. There was a lull before the chaos of the 8:45 a.m. boat-train.

The Sergeant noticed only one traveler loitering among the porters. He involuntarily checked the man's statistics: medium height, fortyish, sallow, dark, anxious. The Sergeant was suddenly interested, and followed when the man slipped into the post office. Smith was in time to overhear the exchange of conversation at the counter. The man spoke with a strong American accent.

It was a lucky week for Sergeant Smith. He had discovered the blotting paper in Macdonnell's rooms and now he was close behind George Bidwell. But he hesitated. The man appeared too short and stocky to fit the description of Warren. And, besides, there was no mention of the name Warren in the telegram which had just been dispatched. It read: "To Mrs. Bidwell, Hotel Victoria, St. Leonards-on-Sea, Kent. Catch the 10:47 a.m. Will meet you at Charing Cross. George." The detective stood aside and let the man leave the post office.

For years George Bidwell had deplored his lack of inches and girth compared to the height and elegance of his younger brother. Now these disadvantages saved him.

There was quite a deputation waiting at the platform barrier when the 10:47 a.m. from St. Leonards drew into Charing Cross at 1:36 p.m. precisely. During the morning Sergeant Smith had become increasingly anxious that he had made a fatal error in allowing George Bidwell to leave the station unaccosted. He had reported his suspicions to headquarters, who were immediately excited. Urgent summons were sent out for two men who knew Frederick Albert Warren by sight. A cashier at the Western Branch of the Bank of England and Mr. Hamilton Green, the Savile Row tailor, hurried off to meet Sergeant Smith at Charing Cross.

George Bidwell was waiting far down the platform. His cold face lit up when the slim figure of Nellie Vernon stepped down from her carriage and he greeted her with unaccustomed effusiveness. The hotel porter, who had accompanied her from St. Leonards, was generously tipped. The luggage was retrieved and the little party moved up the platform. George was nearly through the ticket barrier before Sergeant Smith recognized him.

Heaven knows where George had spent the night, or perhaps he had not gone to bed at all, for he was unshaven and crumpled when the Sergeant had first seen him. Now he was wearing an expensive overcoat and a Sherlock Holmes-type cap. His moustaches were trimmed to half their usual size. But Sergeant Smith noticed the man's anxious eyes.

"That's him," he whispered excitedly. "The man in the black overcoat with the astrakhan collar."

But his companions shook their heads. It was the face of Austin Bidwell they searched for among the jostling crowd. George Bidwell had bilked the authorities once again. Nellie and the luggage were dispatched to her old lodgings at Duke's Road, Euston Square, and George continued with his relentless round of appointments.

It is not difficult to imagine with what eagerness he had perused the newspapers that morning for news of Macdonnell. He learned nothing. With the hope that Macdonnell might still be in town, George visited every rendezvous where Macdonnell might have left a message. Why he was not picked up by the police at one of these mutual haunts passes comprehension.

George was also busy converting some of his English money into more universal currency. A string of jewelers along the Strand did a roaring trade that day. Four diamond lockets, a small gold keyless watch, a fine Brazilian gold necklet, three pearl pins and a turquoise pin in the shape of a parrot, were only a few of the items amid a dowry of jewels which George purchased with his surfeit of sovereigns. He bought a bag at Parkins and Gotto to accommodate these valuables and left it at the shop to be engraved with Nellie's initials.

George was by now too involved to view his situation logically or he would certainly have hesitated before visiting Parkins and Gotto, an exclusive leather shop and stationers in Regent Street which numbered Mr.

and Mrs. Bidwell among their most favored regular customers.

The salesmen, and even Mr. Gotto, had read accounts of the forgeries with particular interest and discussed the similarities between Bidwell and the description of the wanted man. They were fascinated when George walked into the shop two days later, and highly suspicious when he visited them again on Thursday morning. Directly Bidwell left the shop, Mr. Penny, the manager, went to the City Police.

The headquarters at Old Jewry were almost deserted. The manhunt for the forgers had depleted the small force of personnel. The City of London police numbered 780 men, and still retained the ancient right, dating back to 1285, of policing the square mile of the City of London. Intense rivalry existed between this old-established force and the new, much more extensive, Metropolitan Police. It was vital to the pride of the City Police that the forgers should be found, and quickly.

The charges against Noyes were due for a second hearing at the Mansion House the next day. The police were in danger of losing their only suspect unless they could supply enough evidence, bolstered by reliable witnesses, to convince the magistrates that Noyes was implicated in the plot. Every man that could be spared was out on the street, searching.

It was, therefore, excusable, but unfortunate, that Mr. Penny was received with scant enthusiasm when he arrived at Old Jewry. Mr. Penny asked to see the officer in charge of the forgery case and was told that Inspector Bailey was out. He said he was certain the forger had called at his shop that morning, and that he expected him back at the shop at 5 p.m. to collect his bag. The Duty Officer promised to make a note of the fact, but regretted that no steps could be taken until Inspector Bailey returned.

As the day wore on, George Bidwell grew increas-

ingly uneasy. Everywhere he was received with suspicious stares and whispering. A paragraph in the *Daily
Telegraph*, which George had dismissed as wild rumor,
was nevertheless disturbing.

> Yesterday, one of the firm of Messrs. Rothschild,
> accompanied by a detective, visited the prisoner,
> Noyes, and, it was stated, he made some very im-
> portant revelations.

If Noyes had broken down all London now possessed
an accurate description of George Bidwell.

As darkness fell, George entered a hotel cloakroom.
He opened his case and searched among the leather
jewelry cases for his washbag, and extracted his cut-
throat razor and strop. When it was sharpened the
blade cut through the dark stubble on his upper lip
and chin until he was clean-shaven. He packed up his
things again, smiled thinly at his new reflection, and
went out to keep his appointment with Nellie at Marble
Arch.

Still searching for some word from Macdonnell, Nellie
accompanied George on a tour of hotels where she
inquired for a note or a telegram for Mr. Bidwell.

After the fifth fruitless inquiry, Nellie missed her
footing as she climbed back into the cab. As she fell,
her kneecap caught on the iron mounting platform and
she cried out in pain. George clutched her by the fore-
arm and half lifted her into the hansom.

"Watch what you doing another time," he told her
roughly.

Nellie's only answer was a series of short gasps.
George regarded her critically. She hardly represented
the able assistant he required at this crucial stage. There
were tears in her eyes, her short, white teeth bit desperately into her upper lip and a handkerchief twisted
in her nervous fingers. George stretched up and lifted
the small trap-door in the roof.

"Pull up," he shouted loudly to the driver. As the man reined in the horses, George leaned across to Nellie.

"Go home and fetch your landlord," he said. "And join me at Drummond's Hotel."

He climbed out, lifted his hat briefly and dissolved into the darkness.

At 6:30 p.m. he arrived at Drummond's Hotel and booked a private suite in the name of Bidwell. Escape route from the dismal rooms looked unpromising. Green velor curtains in the drawing-room concealed a window with a fifteen-foot drop into the basement area. From the bedroom window a drainpipe offered some purchase against the tiled walls, but it appeared to run down into an enclosed yard.

George picked up a Bradshaw from the bedside table and jotted down departure times of night trains from Euston. Rather than run the gauntlet of an embarkation port, which was almost certain to be watched, he would try to get over to Ireland and catch a boat for New York from there. The Irish Mail left Euston at 9 p.m. for Birmingham, Crewe and Holyhead, with steamer connections to Dublin. George determined to catch it.

Ninety minutes later Nellie had taken the heavy luggage to Euston Station and George had changed into coarse, brown working clothes and heavy lace-up boots. A battered brown bowler hat and Gladstone bag completed the purchases he had made at a second-hand shop round the corner.

George turned and stared across the room at Jules Meunier, Nellie's landlord. He was bent over George's black dressing-case which he was wrestling to close.

"Here, don't ruin it." George brushed the young man out of the way, dragged one of the four canvas bags out of the case, closed the lid and sat on it. The fasteners clicked into their slots.

"Bravo, monsieur!"

George looked up into the dark face and spaniel eyes of Meunier.

"I need help with Nellie and the luggage as far as Holyhead. There is £20 in it if you will come with us."

"Oh, thank you, monsieur, thank you. I will speak to my wife, but she will say yes."

"On the way back pick up the tickets from the station. Two singles to Dublin and one return to Holyhead. And hurry!" George pressed £5 into the Belgian's hand, unlocked the door and propelled him into the corridor. Bidwell's watch said 8:20. Forty minutes to go. He began to gather up the discarded clothes draped over the squat hide chairs. There was a knock on the door, George crossed over and opened it.

What he saw on the other side made his whole body stiffen. He clutched at the door-knob for support.

"Come in," hissed Bidwell. The young salesman from Parkins and Gotto brushed past him into the room.

George closed the door quickly and twisted round with his back against it. So this was it. The police had caught up with him and this youngster was here to establish his identity.

"Well?" he barked.

"The case, I have brought the case," the salesman stammered.

Half an hour ago George had sent a cab-driver to fetch Nellie's bag from Parkins and Gotto. But he had told the man to return alone and bring the case up personally. He took the bag and examined the engraving.

"The workmanship is excellent," he murmured.

There was a hammering on the door.

"Who is it?" shouted George.

"It is I, monsieur!" It was Meunier's voice.

Bidwell let him in. He nodded "Good evening and thank you" to the salesman, pressed a handsome present of gold into his hand and showed him out.

George opened Nellie's case and crammed into it

the boxes of jewelry, the remaining bag of gold, a pair of shoes, a wallet and a nightshirt.

"I must get on ahead," he told Meunier. "Give me my ticket. Here's £20. Take Nellie and the luggage up to Holyhead, book in at the railway hotel and wait for a message." George picked up Nellie's case, his bowler hat and Gladstone bag and fled from the room.

Nellie had reached the top of the main staircase as George turned into the corridor.

"George, George," she shouted. Bidwell paused guiltily and mumbled a few words.

"I don't understand," she answered desperately.

"Meunier will tell you. He is in there." George ran down the empty corridor leading to the service stairs. They were uncarpeted and the nails of his heavy boots clattered from step to step as he raced down two flights. At the bottom he stopped and listened. The silence was eerie. A shaft of light shone through a glass-paneled door on the right, bearing the word "BAR" entwined with vine leaves and grapes. As George opened it and walked in, two men playing cribbage looked up momentarily. He crossed the sawdust floor to the exit, heaved back the heavy brass door-pull and stepped into Drummond Street.

In fact the police were not on Bidwell's tail, despite the efforts of Mr. Penny of Parkins and Gotto. When the cabman had arrived at Parkins and Gotto for Bidwell's bag, Mr. Penny had immediately left to report this fact to the George Street branch of the Metropolitan police, leaving his assistant to take the bag to Bidwell. Mr. Penny explained the situation hastily to the police officer in charge.

Sergeant Hayward stared coldly at Mr. Penny. He sorted through the papers on his desk to find the memo on the forgery case. Carefully he read through the details.

"The name 'Bidwell' has no connection with the

man wanted in the forgery case," he said sharply. "Warren is the man we require for questioning."

Mr. Penny grunted with exasperation. "But I am convinced that this man Bidwell is in fact Warren," he said urgently. "He is at present at Drummond's Hotel, Manchester Square. It is imperative to dispatch detectives there immediately. He said he was leaving town this evening."

The Sergeant shrugged.

"This is a matter for the City Police," he replied coldly. "We cannot interfere."

Next morning Mr. Penny and his assistant composed an indignant letter to the Lord Mayor of London, which received a terse acknowledgement. The young salesman then made a long statement to the Press. This was gleefully printed in all the leading newspapers of March 14th under the heading: "Extraordinary Statement on the Great City Forgeries." Editorials followed condemning the "lack of ordinary vigilance" on the part of the police. Sergeant Hayward was called to Scotland Yard to give reasons why he had not reported Mr. Penny's information. His explanation was not acceptable and he was stripped of his rank.

Dense fog had engulfed the whole of London by 8:25 p.m. on Thursday, March 6th, when Bidwell reached Euston Station. There were three seventy-two-foot archways through the towering portico. The center one was for four-wheeled traffic and the other two were used by pedestrians. The police would be watching the side entrances and also the place where the cabs deposited their passengers, a hundred yards across the station yard.

Standing by the railing at right angles to the portico George knew that the next half-hour would be decisive.

As a mail coach loomed out of the fog, George stepped firmly into the roadway and walked forward behind the vehicle as it moved through the carriage entrance.

Five minutes later Nellie Vernon climbed out of a cab in the station yard. She had at first refused to believe that George would go without her. Now she realized that she was expendable along with the luggage.

Nellie turned to watch Meunier drag a black bag out of the carriage. The bag weighed forty-five pounds and it required all Meunier's strength to lift it off the ground. Nellie was aware that someone was watching her. She looked up and exchanged cold stares with a stranger.

In the busy main hall Nellie and Meunier were impeded by the milling crowds. Nellie noticed the man she had seen in the yard. He was very tall and moving purposefully toward her through the crush of bodies. Meunier was beside her. They were both forced against the wall, surrounded by three men. Curtly, one spoke to Meunier.

"We are police officers. We wish to examine the contents of your bag."

The catches were snapped open, the lid dropped backwards and a hand lifted out a heavy canvas bag. Sergeant Spittle of the City Police fingered the sovereigns inside. Meunier watched in horror.

"But it is not my case, monsieur!" he cried.

"No, no, it belongs to my husband," Nellie protested.

"I arrest you both for being in unlawful possession of this case. Come this way, please."

Heavy hands gripped them as they were propelled through the great hall and hustled into a waiting carriage.

Bidwell lingered amid the yellow fog, 8:40, 8:45, 8:50, the minutes crawled by. His workman's shirt was drenched in sweat. A dozen ominous shapes had solidified out of the murk, but had passed him harmlessly. A match flared in his cupped hands. His fob watch said 8:56. Four minutes to go. Bidwell swallowed nervously. He could hope for no sheltering gloom beneath the glass roofing of the station. The platforms were gaslit. Lifting his cases, he walked boldly into the station.

The slamming of doors along the platform warned passengers on the Irish Mail that departure was imminent.

Bidwell had crossed in front of platform 7 and when a hand touched his jacket sleeve he froze.

"Move over, please. Make way!" A porter shoved Bidwell impatiently to one side. He dragged a trolley-load of luggage to platform 9.

"Gates, gates, only two minutes to go," he shouted, and the ticket-collector left his box to unlock the lug-gate gates.

Bidwell slipped through the platform barrier. And then he ran. A group of shouting women blocked his way to the first carriage, and the second was wide open. Bidwell superstitiously avoided it and yanked open the door of the third compartment. He threw up his cases and scrambled in after them. In the far corner a face looked over a newspaper. The thick neck was enclosed in a dog collar. Bidwell nodded a greeting, turned and pulled the window curtains. Sinking into a corner seat he was almost unconscious when the whistle blew. He fell into an exhausted sleep as the wheels settled into a regular rhythm, eating up the 264 miles to Holyhead.

15

IRELAND
IN A FAST LAP

It was 11 a.m. on Friday, March 7th, and the second Mansion House examination of Edwin Noyes was in full session. The twenty-five-foot-square courtroom was jammed with excited humanity, the rumble of City traffic seeped through the windows on the left of the dais, beneath them were the dark oak benches for counsel. Standing in the front row was the squat, powerfully built figure of Dr. Edward Kenealy. This brilliant Irish advocate, friend of Disraeli and notable champion of forlorn causes, had been briefed for Noyes.

"I strongly protest against my client's case being heard *in camera*," he rasped angrily. "We are not going to have the Inquisition in this country and trying a man *in camera* is a relic of the Inquisition."

Kenealy glared through his pebble glasses at the Lord Mayor of London, Sir Sydney Waterlow, seated beneath the sword of justice sheathed in a red velvet scabbard. Sharply the Lord Mayor looked up. Dr. Kenealy was presumptuous. The Lord Mayor's Court of Justices had been called many things over the years but never an inquisition. He curtly reminded Kenealy of the Lord Mayor's special powers as magistrate under Jervis' Act. Kenealy stared at him scornfully.

"On that theory, any innocent clerk in the City of London is in danger of being summarily arrested, dragged before you in secret session and condemned, unheard, to a week's incarceration in Newgate Prison."

Kenealy paused for the words to sink in. His eyes

swept the crowded public benches opposite. This truculent attitude toward authority made him a favorite with the public. He threw out an arm and pointed a stubby finger at the man in the dock.

"My client has done nothing more than cash genuine checks for his master," Kenealy proclaimed.

Noyes raised his head and looked wildly around the room. Physically he was in a sorry state, his hair was unkempt, his clothes crumpled. Mentally he was clearly almost out of control. During the week Noyes had been interrogated repeatedly but had refused to turn Queen's witness. Eventually, left alone, the inevitable reaction had set in. Realizing that George Bidwell's cast-iron precautions might not save him, he grew so distraught that the warders were afraid he would do himself an injury. Now his desperate eyes searched the faces of the black-gowned aldermen and the Lord Mayor for a grain of hope: Sir Sydney Waterlow was a humane man. He shuffled his papers self-consciously and did not raise his eyes as he replied to Kenealy.

"It is clear from the evidence that the prisoner repeatedly cashed checks of very large sums which were products of the forgeries."

The words were like a death sentence to Noyes. He shrank where he stood.

Colonel Peregrine Madgwick Francis was called to the witness-box, and was followed by five other witnesses. Mr. Freshfield, the Bank of England solicitor, applied to the Bench to have the prisoner remanded for a week; Mr. Kenealy submitted there was no evidence to do any such thing; the Lord Mayor remanded Noyes until Friday week. Noyes had to be helped by two policemen as he stumbled out of the dock.

Unfortunately, Kenealy withdrew from the Bank of England forgery case a few weeks later, when he agreed to lead the defense of the highly controversial Tichborne Claimant. It wrecked his legal career and he grew so passionate for the Claimant's cause that he was disbarred by the Benchers of Gray's Inn.

Later that day Jules Meunier and Ellen Vernon were brought to the Mansion House and appeared before the Lord Mayor. They were both remanded for a week. Nellie had discovered the night before, in the cells at police headquarters in Old Jewry, that she had nothing to gain by shielding George Bidwell. During the following three hours in the interrogating room she told the police about the message Bidwell had promised to leave for her at Holyhead. Two detectives boarded the next Irish mail train out of Euston and picked up the message. In it Bidwell instructed Nellie to proceed to Cork and contact him through the post office. She was to leave a message for him there addressed to Charles Burton.

At 4:30 p.m. on Friday, Bidwell climbed off the train at Cork. The air outside the station was moist and warm, and the mournful hoot of steamers drew him to the river. He crossed the bridge and walked up Patrick Street. Outside the Victoria Hotel he hesitated. The foyer looked rich and welcoming and he was exhausted after twenty hours' traveling. But he was wearing workman's clothes, and moved off instead to the Temperance Hotel in the next street.

Bidwell woke at noon next day. He climbed out of bed and drew back the dingy curtains. It was raining and the pavements were crowded with jostling umbrellas. He was hungry. He dressed quickly and went out to buy a meal and a raincoat.

An hour later Bidwell walked confidently up Grand Parade. He had eaten well and was barely recognizable from a dozen sodden-shoed Irishmen dressed in tweeds, with a cheap ulster round his shoulders and a plaid cap on his head. He congratulated himself that the situation had worked out satisfactorily. He stopped at a letter-box and dropped in a letter addressed to himself under the alias G. C. Brownwell Esq., Brevoort House, Fifth

Avenue, New York. Inside were $17,500 in U.S. bonds. They were emergency funds which he required no longer. The transatlantic steamer berths were only two miles downriver, and he was confident of boarding the ship undetected in his new disguise. Nellie could take the luggage on board separately. He looked at his watch, it was time to contact her.

Bidwell stopped opposite his hotel. He hailed a jaunting car, the Irish one-horse carriage, and asked the cab-driver to drive to the post office and collect Mr. Burton's mail and bring it back to him. As the cabman whipped up his horse, Bidwell crossed the road, paid the bill at the hotel desk and went upstairs to pack.

The cab-driver was a thin, crumbled man with a weather-beaten face. When he reached the post office and asked for Mr. Burton's mail he was seized from both sides and, without a word of explanation, carried kicking and shouting into the street.

A crowd gathered, many of them recognized the cab-driver and the detectives realized there was some mistake. When the man's anger had subsided he explained that he had left Burton at No. 50 Grand Parade.

A police constable on duty overheard the information. He knew Burton was wanted for questioning about the forgeries. To capture the arch-forger single-handed would bring rapid promotion. Pushing his way out of the crowd, he ran off up Oliver Plunkett Street and turned left into Grand Parade. Dashing up the steps of No. 50 he began to hammer on the door with his large red fists.

"Open in the name of the law!" he shouted.

Bidwell was immediately attracted by the noise. He drew back from the window, picked up his suitcase and slipped out of the hotel. Bidwell hailed a carriage in a side-street, climbed in and drew down the window blinds.

Now for the boat. It was unfortunate, but Nellie

would have to fend for herself. He leaned forward to speak to the driver about transatlantic steamer sailings.

"Why, your honor, the next boat to leave Queenstown is the *Cuba,* to be sure. Due at three o'clock tomorrow, the Sabbath, and a fine day for traveling."

So there were twenty-four hours to kill. It had been too much to hope a boat would be ready at the dockside, and about to sail that very afternoon. Twenty-four hours meant another night's lodging. Bidwell did not intend to remain in Cork, and offered the driver a small fortune to convey him to Lismore, twenty miles to the north-east.

The constable who had disturbed the occupants of No. 50 Grand Parade was given a severe reprimand. The forger might have been taken if plain-clothes detectives had followed discreetly behind the driver to his rendezvous with Burton. As it was, a frantic search of every hotel in Cork produced nothing, no suspicious characters were lingering around the docks, but when two smartly dressed young men stepped off the Dublin train that evening they were instantly arrested and flung into Bridewell Prison.

At 9 p.m. that evening Bidwell booked into the Lismore House Hotel for the night. During the long and uproarious drinking session at a small inn on the road, Bidwell had plied the cabman with strong doses of poteen, so that on his return to Cork he would be too fuddled to reply to police questioning.

After dinner Bidwell visited the residents' lounge in search of a newspaper. The only occupant was seated in one of the velvet upholstered chairs round the log fire. He was reading a newspaper. The only newspaper, Bidwell discovered, as he rummaged among the magazines on a circular table in the middle of the room. He chose a copy of *Punch* at random and sat down beside the fire.

"Good evening." The man opposite looked up briefly and returned to his paper.

"Good evening." Bidwell stared at the man idly. He was about forty, with a long wedge-shaped face and yellowish complexion. A lawyer, or a doctor, perhaps. Bidwell despised the professional classes. He lay back appreciatively in the chair. The fire warmed his legs and the oil lamps on the tables cast an intimate and friendly glow.

"Would you join me in a whiskey nightcap?" The man had finished reading and turned amicably to Bidwell.

"Thank you."

"I missed you on the evening train," he said, turning the brass bell-handle by the fireplace.

"I traveled down yesterday," Bidwell replied.

"From Dublin?"

Bidwell hesitated. Perhaps the man knew the city intimately.

"No, through from London," he answered.

A small frown of concentration appeared between the lawyer's hard blue eyes.

"You have business at the Castle?" he queried.

"No," said Bidwell.

"You are a Yankee?" The tone of this question sent a warning spiral of anxiety up Bidwell's backbone.

"Yes," he answered coldly.

The waiter put a salver on the table between the guests. The heavy, cut-glass tumblers sparkled with reflected light. The lawyer drank his whiskey and picked up the paper again. Bidwell turned the pages of his magazine. His nose twitched from the smell of danger.

The lawyer re-read the news about the Bank of England forgeries but could find no description of the wanted man. Perhaps he could surprise his fellow guest to give himself away. Suddenly he lurched forward, thrusting the paper in front of Bidwell's face.

"Do you wish to read the paper?" he challenged.

Bidwell stared at the page "GREAT CITY FORGERIES," he read. "Yesterday, Edwin Noyes, twenty-six years of age, an American, was brought before the Lord Mayor . . ." He dragged his eyes away.

"I do not read the *Telegraph,*" he answered coldly.

The man threw down the paper and stood up.

" I take it you are staying tonight?" he asked.

"Yes, yes. See you at breakfast. Good night."

"Good night." The lawyer walked purposefully out of the room. He would speak to the police before breakfast next day.

Directly the door-latch clicked back into place, Bidwell dived for the paper. If he hoped to read that Noyes had been released through lack of evidence he was disappointed. The report covered a column and a half, and in the final paragraphs he read of Nellie's arrest. Nellie taken! Bidwell stared blankly into the fire, the paper fell into a crumpled heap on the floor. Could the girl conceivably keep her mouth shut? There rose before him the memory of a policeman battering on the door of No. 50 Grand Parade. No—the game was up. The perfect crime was splintered into a thousand fragments. He sat immobile for half an hour.

Then, swallowing down his whiskey, he went to bed.

He slept badly and woke when early morning changed the color of the uncurtained windows from black to soupy gray. He got up and dressed in the half-light, stared a moment at his suitcase then kicked it carefully under the bed. The bill was not paid and he dare not leave the hotel with luggage in his hand. He opened the bedroom door with his boots cradled in his arms and crept down the stairs.

There was no one in the hall and a heavy iron key had been left in the front-door lock. Bidwell let himself out and slid like a shadow along the deserted street. He found some stables, hired a cab and was rattling out of the ancient and picturesque little town of Lismore soon after dawn. The lawyer had missed his prey.

The Cunard Royal Mail steamer *Cuba* was searched

from stem to stern before it sailed from Queenstown harbor that afternoon, but no one was apprehended.

Bidwell had slipped back to Dublin. He stayed at the Cathedral Hotel that night and was out early on the streets in search of a paper boy. He bought a pile of newspapers. It was just as he feared. There was a reward of £500 on his head and an accurate description of his appearance and dress. He had been traced as far as Cork when the English papers went to press. That was twelve hours ago.

The police were close behind him now. He must find a new disguise. Bidwell boarded a tramcar and got off on the outskirts of the town. The Tuesday street market was in full swing. Bidwell pushed his way through a crowd of women with black shawls and rush baskets, arguing the price of potatoes. The clothes stalls were further down.

It took Bidwell half an hour to find what he required among the hanging lines of topcoats, suits and ulsters. Tangled piles of shirts and underclothes, hats, gloves and boots lay on tables. Bidwell sorted through them, putting aside those he required. He carried his purchases into the men's lavatory on the corner.

Bidwell stooped to unlace his boots and stepped out of them on to the damp floor. His tweed trousers were replaced by a pair of tight black breeches. He slipped into a dark, wasp-waisted topcoat, settled a top-hat firmly on his head and drew on a pair of calf gloves. Bidwell's impersonation of a Frenchman might deceive the Irish police. He spoke the language well enough and an assumed accent would obliterate the give-away American twang which plagued his English conversation. He transferred his wallet to the new coat and stuffed his old suit and ulster into a black valise.

It was then that he noticed the white silk scarf was missing. With a shock of dismay he remembered he had left it on the hook behind the Dublin hotel bedroom door. It had been Nellie's Christmas present to him. The initials G.B. were embroidered on the corner. If the hotel management had found the scarf and pieced together the circumstances of his late arrival and precipitate departure they would inevitably call the police. It would be madness to remain in Dublin. But where else could he go? He dare not try to board a transatlantic steamer, yet to return to England was unthinkable. Carefully his racing brain sought for a hole in the closing gap. Scotland! Scotland was his only hope of refuge. He could hide in Glasgow or Edinburgh until the hue and cry had died away, and then make a bolt for home from a Scottish port.

The night boat from Belfast to Glasgow might not be watched by the police. If it was he would have to rely on bluff and his new disguise to get him on board. He must catch a train to Belfast immediately. Bidwell took a small bottle from his pocket and swallowed down two stomach pills. He picked up his black valise and, summoning the remainder of his overtaxed tenacity and nerve, set out for the station.

16

THE
DOUBLE BACK

Behind the long mahogany counter of the buffet-room in Dublin station a waitress was polishing glasses, but her attention was held by two men sitting by the window.

The waitress had noticed them come into the buffet directly it opened and that was five hours ago. They were clean, good-looking fellows wearing identical raincoats and hats. The men were staring out of the window. Their presence gave a disquieting atmosphere to the usually cheerful buffet-room.

From the window the two men had an uninterrupted view of the principal section of the platform. But a row of slot machines jutting out from the wall obstructed the view to the ticket barrier. In the protected corner, between the slot machines and the ticket-collector's cabin, three iron railway benches had been placed for the convenience of passengers. When Bidwell walked on to the platform he immediately noticed the benches and seated himself on one of them, shielded by an open newspaper. As the through train from Cork steamed into the station Bidwell folded his newspaper and walked toward the train. Simultaneously the two detectives emerged from the buffet and moved swiftly along the platform. As the men drew level with him, Bidwell expelled the air from his lungs in an audible gasp. Hearing the sound, the detectives hesitated and glanced sharply round at the strange figure in the silk top-hat. But the carriage doors had opened and passengers were climbing out. The detectives had strict instructions to examine every man who passed through the exit off the Cork train. As they took up their positions on either side of the barrier, one spoke to the ticket-collector.

"Who is that man over there in the top-hat?" he asked.

"Oh, he is a Frenchman. Doesn't speak a word of English. I even had to count out the money for his ticket for him."

Bidwell was boarding the train. He sat down, alert to the sound of the porters hammering down the couplings between the carriages. He watched the guard pass his window on the way down the train. A whistle blew and the train began to move slowly forward.

Having failed to identify their man among the disembarking Cork passengers, the detectives resumed their vigil in the station buffet.

When the train reached Belfast it had grown dark. After the commotion on the platform had died away, and the carriages had been dragged backward to the engine-shed, an excited porter, who had carried Bidwell's case from the train to a cab, fetched his bicycle, lit the oil wheel-light and pedaled fast down the road to the police station.

Around seven o'clock the cab carrying George Bidwell clattered along the broad, cobbled quayside and drew up opposite the Glasgow steamer berth. Bidwell paid off the driver and moved swiftly into the indigo shadows of the warehouse.

There was a smell of salt and seaweed. It was two hours before the boat was due to sail and the whole area appeared deserted. A fresh wind from the north had swept away the rain and the velvet ceiling of the sky was torn with jagged stars. The only sounds were the fat slap, slap of the water against the harbor wall and the groan of the retaining ropes of the steamer as they tightened and relaxed their embrace of the giant, stone bollards on the quay. Storm lanterns, at the mast head of the ship, sent marching pools of light across the empty deck as they swung softly with the tilting ship.

Bidwell's eyes could not penetrate the deep shadows cast by the cranes hanging motionless beside the ship. Would the police step forward to the gangway when he reached the deck of the ship and effectively cut off his only escape route? He would have to risk it.

The gang-plank chains rattled sharply as he stepped on to the boards and a startled seagull screamed in protest from the rigging. Bidwell tripped on the step-down to the ship's deck, clutched at the gangway rope to steady himself, and a cast a fugitive glance behind him along the quay. All was silent as before.

When Bidwell had roused the purser from his ledger books and obtained a ticket he crossed to the door marked "Gentlemen." He had cut away the stubble of three days' growth of whiskers and was trimming a thin pencil-line moustache on his upper lip when his eyes widened. He could hear the sound of hurried foot-steps clattering down the brass-bounded stairs of the main companionway. In one swift movement he lunged to the door and softly turned the brass handle. He eased the door open a crack and listened tensely to a man's voice speaking abruptly.

"Purser, a cab has just brought a man from the Dublin train. Where is he?"

"Oh, you mean the Frenchman. He is over in the washroom."

Bidwell's blood curdled, but he recovered instantly. When the washroom door was wrenched open Bidwell was back in his place in front of the handbasin. The top-hat was placed exactly on his head, as he flicked the dust from his lapel. In the mirror he stared in insolent surprise at the two men who had so violently interrupted his ablutions.

"Pardon me," the senior detective muttered instinctively as a strong whiff of scent reached his nostrils. The two men stared hard at the bizarre figure, then backed out, closing the door softly behind them.

Bidwell did not relax the iron grip on his nerves for the whole of the next two hours. He wandered in a dream through the lower decks which grew congested with passengers and porters, with white-coated waiters and seamen in high boots and oilskins.

At last he heard the shouts of the sailors on the top deck, the clang and clatter of the gangways being unchained and the first throb of the marine engines in the bowels of the ship. The tension in his stomach unwound and he dashed back to the washroom where he was violently sick. Then he found his way to his cabin and did not emerge until the ship docked in Glasgow next morning.

But one of the cabins remained empty all through the voyage. Its would-be occupant had been arrested on the gangplank before the ship sailed, on suspicion of connection with the bank forgery. Twelve other innocent citizens were arrested in Belfast that evening.

London police headquarters received reports of these false arrests with irritation. The over-enthusiasm of the Irish police only increased the furore in the newspapers and their own embarrassment.

Two more Scotland Yard detectives were sent to reinforce the two men already based in Cork. This picked force arrested a man on March 13th in a Queenstown billiard-room who answered exactly to the description of George Bidwell. He was released the next day. On March 18th two men and a woman were picked up in the Cork Provincial Bank and another arrest was made on the outskirts of the city, but none of these individuals had any connection with the crime.

"The police are looking wildly about them, apparently without the remotest notion which way to turn," the *City Press* commented on March 15th. The police had completely lost the scent of George Bidwell in the water jump between Ireland and Scotland and had not the slightest notion that he was hidden away in Edinburgh.

Two weeks after the discovery of the forgeries the principal miscreants remained unaccounted for. The Bank of England began to grow seriously alarmed and decided to take matters into their own hands. Telegrams were sent off to their legal representatives in all the leading cities of the world, instructing them to keep a sharp lookout for the criminals. A special cable was dispatched to Messrs. Seward, Blachford, Griswold and Da Costa, Solicitors to the Bank of England in New York, giving them full responsibility to work on the case. This firm immediately gave instructions to Pinkertons, the world-famous private detective agency.

Big Bill Pinkerton, six foot four in his socks, called his ablest assistant into his office in 66 Exchange Place, New York.

"Good morning, Curtin," Pinkerton looked up at the compact, assertive figure of John Curtin entering the room. He waved at a chair opposite his desk.

"Sit down." Pinkerton stubbed out his cigar and reached for a clean, brown folder lying on top of a pile of other papers. "I want you to drop everything. Something urgent has come in. It's the Bank of England case."

Curtin's eyes widened as Pinkerton opened the folder and picked out a single sheet of paper inside.

"The Bank of England wish to know the true identity of Warren. Here are the facts."

Curtin took the paper and carefully read through the description furnished by Colonel Francis of Austin Bidwell. Beneath the pen portrait only two further details were supplied—"American" and "Familiar with the workings of high finance."

Pinkerton took another cigar from his case and lit it, waiting for Curtin's reaction.

"He must have trained in a large city. Chicago or New York," Curtin deduced.

"Yes," Pinkerton shook out his match and dropped it in the large brass ashtray. "Get down to Wall Street and see what you can find."

"Yes, sir." Curtin stood up, folded the sheet of paper carefully into his notebook and walked swiftly out of the room.

17

HONEYMOONING
WITH FATE

Shifting uncomfortably in the straw, Austin Bidwell raised himself on one elbow and looked round. Light shone from a single hurricane lamp hooked to a rusty nail on a crossbeam two feet overhead. It illumined the wooden rafters, bales of straw, iron mangers. The noise was deafening. A blizzard raged, hurling itself against the deserted barn which Austin and his wife and their servant had found as shelter for the night. The doors bulged and creaked, wind screamed through the cracks in the wooden walls. Austin shivered and drew his overcoat closer round his shoulders.

Ten paces across the earth floor a bullock moved restlessly. The confounded beast had cost him a fortune when he bought it off a passing carrier after the Paris to Madrid express came to a halt. The Carlist rebels had informed bewildered passengers that the railway tracks had been ripped up throughout the next twenty-five-mile section.

With his wife, servant and luggage, Austin had set off southward by bullock cart, reckoning to reach civilization by dusk. But the road bridges had been blown and telegraph wires were down. Now they were cut off from the outside world, wandering in the foothills of the Pyrenees, trapped in the chaos of a civil war.

Austin looked at his watch, it was already six o'clock. Despite the blizzard they must move on at dawn. He would have to catch the boat which left for Cadiz in ten days' time.

Some days later the little party struggled into Burgos. Trains were still running south. There was time to reach Cadiz before the boat sailed. They sold the bullock and cart and boarded the Madrid train. But at Avila the signals were up. Passengers were ordered on to the platform. Martial law had been proclaimed and rolling stock was commandeered for troop transportation.

Austin strode to the telegraph office. He sent off telegrams to Government officials, the president of the railway and superintendent of the district. He offered prayers, threats and huge sums in cash for transport over the sixty miles to Madrid. He reached Madrid, 300 miles from Cadiz, on the day the boat was due to sail. Frantically he telegraphed the agents to hold the boat. His request was refused.

Dashing to the shipping office, Austin thumbed through the steamship timetables. A French steamer was due at Santander on March 1st to pick up passengers and mail before continuing to Mexico. Austin shepherded his little flock all the way back to Santander.

Thankfully he closed the book on his disastrous Spanish sojourn and went aboard the *Martinique* at Santander.

By March 15th the French steamer had ploughed westward for fifteen days, only touching in at St. Thomas to refuel. Austin swung his legs down from the bunk, crossed to the porthole and peered out. Cuba, pearl of the Antilles, slashed a jagged line of yellow between the glittering blue of the sea and the sky. Fascinated, he watched the boat approach a beach of silver sand which grew larger until he could detect the final ripples of the sea making half-hearted rushes up the shore. The deserted bay was fringed with palm trees, their elephantine trunks topped by feather-duster heads which danced in the trade wind. Here was the perfect spot for a honeymoon! Austin turned from the window and began to dress. The ship's steering bell clanged and the *Martinique* turned for Havana. There were fresh provisions to be loaded before the final three-day run to Mexico.

In fifteen minutes Austin was clothed in a white drill suit. Everything was white from boater to canvas shoes. The sun had burnt a warmth into his sallow skin, emphasizing his ruthless good looks. Austin adjusted his diamond tiepin and picked up his white sun umbrella.

The glare blinded him momentarily when he stepped on to the desk. And then he saw Havana, a collection of white houses huddled on a spit of land trapped in the glittering sea.

Jane turned from the deck-rail. Austin squeezed her hand, smiling down at her excited face while onlookers gazed in admiration. They made an attractive couple. He spoke to his servant.

"Oh, Nunn, we are disembarking here. Please attend to the luggage. My wife and I will go ahead to the principal hotel in town."

"Disembark in Havana, sir?" Nunn had understood his master was in frantic haste to reach Mexico. And surely he knew that a civil war was raging in Cuba.

"Here are the trunk and suitcase keys, Nunn." The man took them and disappeared down the companionway.

"How wonderful, Austin, are we really to land here?"

"Yes." Austin grinned wickedly. "Our second honeymoon."

He knew it would be wise to proceed at once to Mexico. To live there quietly for two years, away from the limelight, safe in some peaceful hacienda in the mountains. But now the dream approached reality he shied away. Challenge, action, achievement, these were words that Austin loved and understood. A fighting man, eager for battle, he dreaded inactivity and boredom.

A Negro porter from the Hotel Telegrapho escorted the Bidwells ashore, and hired a gig to drive his charges up through the narrow streets of the old town. The road was twisting and congested, a smell of tobacco filled the air. Reaching the tree-lined avenues of the modern city, they dismounted beneath the striped awning of the Hotel Telegrapho in the main square. That evening visiting and invitation cards were presented at their room. But before joining the social roundabout Jane had to see a doctor and Austin wanted to catch up on the world Press news.

Back in New York, Captain John Curtin had completed some adroit detective work. He had made the rounds of the brokers' offices on Wall Street, and in three days had collected a list of twenty men who might have been connected with such a crime as the forgery case. It took twenty-four hours to account for sixteen of them. He made minute inquiries about the remaining four, and singled out Austin Bidwell as the most suspicious candidate. Curtin interviewed the men who knew Bidwell. One remembered Austin saying he would settle in the tropics when he was rich. Twenty-four hours later Curtin stepped off the train at Key West, Florida. He booked into a rooming house in the town and began a search of the surrounding islands for signs of Austin Bidwell.

Next evening Austin let himself quietly into his hotel suite. He was hot, and the vast room, paved with white marble, looked cool and refreshing. Shadows from the barred windows striped the sunlit floor and climbed over the carved, lace-covered bed. It had been a tiresome day. Early that morning Austin had picked up a discarded New York paper in a curbside café and read that Noyes was arrested and the hunt was on for Warren. He retraced his steps up through the fetid streets of the old town, convinced there was nothing to connect his name with any notorious forger. But as a precaution he would leave for Mexico immediately and adopt an alias. Knowing he could not change his name without his wife's connivance, he regarded her warily across the room, hoping to achieve his object with his usual potent mixture of half-truth and flattery. She looked pliable enough, dressed only in a thin, white petticoat; there was a book in her hand, but she had been watching through the jalousies of the window for his return.

"Austin, listen," she said urgently. "I must tell you, I am going to have a baby."

The smile froze on his face. Nervously, his agile mind examined this further complication.

"Are you sure?" he asked her.

"Yes, isn't it wonderful? The doctor told me," she said.

"I am so glad," he lied. "A child of my own." Suddenly he felt exhausted. "I think I have a touch of the sun," he said, his hand pressed to his face. He turned away, tugging off his cravat.

"I must rest," he said, and threw himself fully clothed on to the bed.

She perched on the bed and stroked his hair softly, chattering on about her interview with the doctor. Austin lay with his eyes closed, halfway to sleep. Suddenly he was wide awake.

"What did you say?" he queried, opening his eyes.

"The doctor says an American has robbed the Bank of England of half a million pounds!"

So she had heard. He glanced at her tentatively.

"Sounds a pretty smart American," he said. "I hope he gets away with it."

"On the contrary, I think he should be horse-whipped," she answered angrily.

It was the same elderly doctor who picked up his ebony cane and walked down through the flower-scented streets to the post office. He was accompanied by a slave who trotted along the gutter, shielding the doctor from the sun with a large, green parasol. The doctor had received a cable from a man he imagined was a journalist, requesting the names of any prominent Americans who had lately arrived on the island. The doctor addressed his reply to John Curtin, c/o Poste Restante, Key West, Florida, and the name he supplied was Austin Bidwell.

18

HOST
LEAVES FIRST

The crash of the evening gun on the guardship in the harbor echoed across the bay. It was March 20th and the sun was setting on another serenely beautiful day in Havana. Cranes were still working by the harbor wall, loading luggage on to the Mexican steamer which was due to sail that evening. But none of the trunks belonged to Austin Bidwell. Captivated by the exuberance of high life in Havana, he had postponed his departure from the island.

Cuba had long been a paradise for Spaniards with energy and ambition. Huge fortunes were easily made and Austin at once appreciated their expertise and luxurious mode of life. Brushing caution aside, he ripped open some Bank of England thousand-sovereign bags and flung himself into the social whirl. It was a disastrously reckless move.

As the last reverberation of the gun explosion died away, Bidwell strode into the banqueting-room of the Hotel Telegrapho. He wore tropical evening dress and a purple cummerbund; his shirt-front glittered with diamonds.

Members of some of the leading Creole families were dining with Austin that night. Creoles were second- and third-generation pure-bred Spaniards, who had made Cuba their home. Enjoying his role as host of the evening, Austin watched the preparations possessively. Dark-skinned waiters hurried through the swing doors with glasses, cutlery and china. Giant branched candela-

bra were placed down the center of the table and the
hundred candles lit. Austin pulled out his cigar-case.
As a waiter applied a taper to his cigar, the flame reflected in Austin's small eyes, the pupils bright with
self-pride.

Suddenly the hubbub of the dining-room was interrupted by the screech of an "All aboard" klaxon from
the harbor. Bidwell expelled a lungful of smoke, and
listened imperturbably. He was not to know that as
the steamer for Mexico nosed out of the bay it passed
the *Morro Castle,* one of the twice-weekly packets arriving from New York and Key West, with Captain
John Curtin aboard.

Three hours later the banquet was nearly over. Austin
leaned back in the huge, gold-embossed, leather armchair at the head of the table. He gestured for the fruit
and finger-bowls to be removed and the port to be circulated, then turned to continue his flirtation with the
Creole beauty on his right.

As a clock chimed a quarter to eleven there was a
sound of marching feet in the square below. A curt order
cracked through the warm air and the footsteps halted.
Conversation in the banqueting-room faded into silence.
Jane Bidwell glanced anxiously at her guests. Each
waited for the next sound. In 1868, and again in 1871,
there had been massacres in the Plaza de Mars when
students had paraded the blue and white flag of Cuba
and sung freedom songs. Mansions of some of the leading Creole families in the city had been overrun by
Spanish militia and the contents smashed to pieces. The
moments ticked by.

Everyone turned as the wide arched door of the banqueting-room opened slowly. Everyone but Austin Bidwell. Three civilians stood there: the British Vice-Consul, an aide-de-camp of the Captain-General of Cuba,
and John Curtin. The men conferred briefly and Curtin
walked forward, stopping close to Austin's chair.

"I would like to speak to you, Austin Bidwell, if you

would step outside." Curtin's voice was flat and no emotion showed in his cold face.

Bidwell seemed not to hear him.

"Outside, if you please," Curtin repeated.

Austin's brain clicked back into action. He placed his napkin on the table and spoke blandly to his guests.

"Ladies and gentlemen, pray excuse me for a moment."

Halfway to the door he stopped deliberately. If he spoke quietly he would not be overheard by the civilians at the door or his guests at the table.

"Now what's the trouble," he asked sharply.

"Mr. Bidwell, I have a warrant in my pocket for your arrest upon the charge of forgery upon the Bank of England."

"But I am an American citizen. Surely you know that. There is no law under which you can arrest me in Cuba." Austin spoke coolly, but his eyes challenged the detective. And Curtin knew that Austin was correct.

"The warrant is signed by the Captain-General of Cuba. I am John Curtin of Pinkerton's Detective Agency, and you are my prisoner," he replied.

"What you propose is completely illegal," Austin told him furiously.

"We will discuss that question later, Mr. Bidwell," Curtin said.

There was one more line to take. It was a slim chance, but worth trying.

"Mr. Curtin," Austin muttered, "I have $15,000 in my case. It is yours if you will let me go alone to my room to collect it."

"I'm sorry, Mr. Bidwell, bribery is not in my line."

The guests had begun to murmur, now one half-rose from his chair.

"Do you need help, Bidwell?" he shouted across.

Curtin's eyes narrowed. "If you do not come quietly I will have to call up the military from below," he said.

Austin turned back to his guests, searching his mind

for an excuse, a cause for imprisonment with honor. He stared along the double row of dark-tanned faces turned toward him.

"There has been an unhappy mistake, gentlemen," he told them. "I am arrested upon a charge of supplying arms to the insurrectionists in the eastern provinces."

"Austin, how dare they? It's a monstrous lie!"

His wife! He had forgotten Jane. The girl had half risen from her chair, determined to defend him. Clutching the table edge, he leaned forward, hurling the words toward her.

"Don't say a word about who you are, what you are, where you are from or anything about us," he commanded, and walked swiftly out of the room.

With mumbled excuses the guests began to rise, their few hours' allegiance to their hostess ended.

Left in blank-faced isolation among the empty chairs, Jane became aware of a man's voice.

"I am the British Vice-Consul. I believe you are a British subject. I am here to help you all I can."

The Bidwells' room and luggage was searched. Nothing was found except a notebook with some leaves torn out, but when the British Vice-Consul left the Hotel Telegrapho in the early hours of March 21st, he carried with him $5,000 in United States notes which he had persuaded Mrs. Bidwell to disclose.

That morning the Bank of England heard the glad news that Warren had been arrested and $5,000 of the proceeds of the fraud recovered. Mrs. Bidwell was under surveillance at a hotel and the servant, Henry Nunn, was behind bars.

The arrests had been swift and arbitrary, though their legality was doubtful. No law existed by which an American citizen could be arrested, following a request made by the British Government, to the Spanish authorities in Madrid, and detained in a Cuban military prison. Bidwell was therefore kept strictly confined and no one was allowed to visit him until the legal situation had been straightened out.

News of the arrest caused uproar in Havana. Distinguished lawyers in the city pronounced it "utterly illegal," "completely unjustified" and "without precedent." No one appeared to care whether Bidwell was guilty or not. The Cubans saw his incarceration as a typical example of Colonial oppression, where the rights of the individual were squashed by the high-handed behavior of the Spanish Captain-General.

The *New York Herald* correspondent leapt to Austin's defense. Daily he telegraphed inflamed articles to the mainland which were printed with banner headlines: "International Complication in Consequence of the Bank of England Forgeries," "Colonial Outrages in Common and Treaty Law," "Bidwell, the Prisoner, an American and Native of Indiana." "The arrest is in violation of the laws of Spain and of treaty stipulations with the United States and in contempt of the guarantees of the law of 1870." Complaints were made that $5,000 had been obtained by compulsion from Mrs. Bidwell.

After seven days the protests had grown so virulent that a lawyer was admitted to Austin Bidwell. Through him Austin immediately threatened an action for illegal arrest. He demanded aid from Mr. Torbert, the American Consul, who hastily cabled Washington for instructions. On April 3rd the U.S. Consul demanded the release of the prisoner Bidwell, alias Warren, from the Cuban authorities, on the grounds that he was a U.S. citizen. The British Consul strenuously opposed the move. Before Bidwell was set free the Bank of England lawyers in New York were able to push through an attachment against Bidwell for £100,000 ($497,760 gold). It was signed by Judge Faucher of the American Supreme Court. The Bank of England had won the first round, Bidwell was now legally confined.

The next stage was extradition. There was no extradition treaty between Spain and either England or America, and Austin Bidwell insisted that he be extradited to New York. The lawyers argued and arbitrated. But on April 10th Mr. Fish, United States Secretary of State, gave authority for Austin Bidwell to be handed over to the British police, provided they could produce sufficient proof of his guilt and he could be fully identified.

Desperation made Austin act. Soon after dawn next morning a sentry parading the length of Havana Military Prison picked up a pair of white canvas shoes. He delivered them to the duty officer who ordered an immediate check on the prisoners. The guard who unlocked Austin's cell found it empty. The door on to the balcony had been forced, and a torn scrap of white silk hung from a nail protruding from the balcony railing.

News of the escape was received with satisfaction in the city. A judge voiced the general feeling when he asserted that it was better for the prisoner to escape than that he should be delivered to a foreign power, thus establishing such a bad precedent. A reward of $500 was offered for his recapture.

It was after midnight when the brilliant notion of escape struck Austin Bidwell.

He was lying helpless on a straw palliasse in his small cell. The only light filtered through a peephole in the door to the corridor. But there was another door which opened on to the balcony. As a favored prisoner, he used it for exercise each day.

Made of stout wood, it was kept locked. Standing close up to the door, he lunged at it with his shoulder. It burst open! It was too easy, he was virtually free. Austin did not hesitate. He invariably acted on impulse, relying on his own sharp wits to take advantage of ensuing situations. Tugging on his canvas shoes, he slid into the fresh air.

Bidwell's cell, facing north, was part of the huge

oblong façade of the prison which dominated the head-land. Beyond the parade ground there was only sea.

The cell was on the second story. In his mind's eye Bidwell measured the distance to the ground; fourteen, sixteen, even eighteen feet. But he was six feet tall, and his arms, outstretched, would add another three. Quite a fall on to the hard-packed sand of the parade ground. He groped for the balcony rail and swung one long leg over, then twisted round and tried to wedge his foot into one of the spaces between the upright supports of the balcony. The space was too narrow, he would have to remove his shoes. He climbed back and pulled them off. Then leaned and dropped them over the railings. Guards were supposed to patrol the prison, but after the midnight changeover their heavy footsteps were rarely heard until dawn.

This time his toes found a temporary purchase on the crumbling stonework between the railings. He swung the other leg over and gingerly bent down to clutch an upright with one hand. So far it was easy. All his weight was poised above the balcony rail. He must now swing his body outward, let go with his feet, hoping he would get a purchase with the other hand as he fell.

He hesitated—and then stepped out into nothing. It was the nail that saved him. The balconies were built flush with the prison walls and nails had been driven in to connect the iron with the stonework. This nail was rusty and protruded half an inch. It had hooked into the upper sleeve of Austin's shirt as he pressed against the wall for support. When he threw out his weight, it ripped the sleeve from armpit to wrist and tore a jagged wound in his skin, but it steadied him for a second before the cuff of the shirt tore off. When it did he used his hand to steady his weight again, then crashed to the ground.

Pain screamed through him. The flesh of his hands and knees was crushed and bruised as he hit the sand. Austin flung himself on to his back, rocking to and fro with pain. Slowly, the agony receded. He must get moving quickly. Anxiously he flexed his legs, nothing appeared to be broken. Using his untorn knuckles as support, he heaved himself on to his feet. Swiftly he checked his position. The gaunt pile of the prison lay behind him, across the parade ground the spidery arm of the garrotting tree yawned into the sky. Austin smiled grimly. The last eleven men to break out of prison had all been recaptured and shot at a public execution. He staggered a few steps, then broke into a run across the hard-packed sand. His breath came quick and frantic as he reached the perimeter of the parade ground, and stumbled across a rutted, dusty road. There before him was the wonderful wide sea, with a fringe of creamy breakers lapping the rocky shore of the island. He ran the length of the curving esplanade, then paused again for breath. Austin turned off the road and down a sandy track by the shore. His hands throbbed painfully, blood congealed on his knees, making them stiff and sore. His head ached and panic began to creep through his brain. He was heading toward the deserted, swampy western sector of the island. His only practical chance of survival was to steal a boat from a busy harbor and sail the hundred miles across the Straits of Florida to the American mainland, or to join the Cuban rebels in the eastern mountains. The rising sun found Austin staggering forward to nowhere.

For two days he wandered on and it was April 14th when the London *Daily Telegraph* reported a cable from Havana:

Authority has once more laid hands on Austin Bidwell. Bruised and injured in person and clothing he has been recaptured on the seashore twenty miles above Havana.

To implement the extradition order two City of London detectives had already left for Cuba, accompanied by Mr. John Good, a cashier at the Western Branch of the Bank of England, who would identify Austin Bidwell as F. A. Warren.

On April 14th Bidwell was formally handed over to the British Consul, who put him in charge of the detectives. They also took possession of $7,000 in U.S. bonds, three diamond studs, a pair of gold and amethyst cufflinks, and a gold watch-chain and seal comprising two ships, three crossed martlets and four fishes.

At dusk on May 27th Austin and Jane Bidwell, Captain John Curtin, Detective Sergeants Michael Haydon and William Green, and Mr. Good landed at Plymouth off the steamer *Moselle*. Bidwell was given ten minutes to say goodbye to his wife before catching the train to London. At 4:35 a.m. next morning he walked through the gates of Newgate Prison to join Edwin Noyes.

19

THE
BOARDING PARTY

The revenue cutter *Seneca,* fastest launch in New York harbor, tore across the choppy water of the bay while Captain Irving, head of the New York detectives, and his assistant Inspector Philip Farley clung to the safety rail and prayed for speed. Under cover of the screeching engines they considered how to shake off Deputy Sheriff Judson Jarvis, who had refused to be left ashore. Irving staggered unsteadily across to speak to the quarantine authorities in the bows.

The other policeman gazed back along the creamy wake of the *Seneca*. They had pulled away from the pursuing launch, which was occasionally visible as it bucketed up and down in the swell. The throttle of the second boat was fully open, for the occupants were as anxious as the police to be first aboard the giant liner.

Sitting up in bed in his cabin on S.S. *Thuringia*. Macdonnell closed his wallet and placed it on his breakfast tray. It was reassuring to discover he had £7,000 in hand. This would be ample to iron out any obstacles which might arise about his safe conduct to the shore. Macdonnell felt the jolt as the ship nudged against the quarantine boat. He twisted round and lifted the corner of his pillow. Slipping into his pocket the small-caliber pistol which lay there, he picked up his gold watch and chain, glancing at the time. It was 9:30 a.m. on Thursday, March 20th, and he was nearly home.

There was a sharp rap on the door. Macdonnell swung his legs out of bed and crossed the room. As he opened the door, the falsely smiling face of Inspector Philip Farley became visible.

Macdonnell was relieved. He had written to Farley from Europe, requesting him to meet the ship, and enclosing a preliminary bribe of $400.

"Please come in," Macdonnell said, opening the door wide.

Farley pushed past Macdonnell into the cabin. He was out of breath from scrambling up the ship's accommodation ladder. Irving had climbed up after him, but when Deputy Sheriff Judson Jarvis made to follow he was obstructed. The Medical Officer of Health reminded the Sheriff of the ruling that no one was allowed on board a liner until it had been cleared for quarantine.

Macdonnell closed the door.

"How delightful to see you, Inspector. So you received my letter and small donation of respect?"

Farley nodded briefly. His hard blue eyes stared coldly at Macdonnell, his heavy body seemed to fill the cabin.

"Your pistol," he snapped.

"Come, come, Inspector, you're not afraid of me." Macdonnell pulled the pistol from his pocket, and tossed it lightly on to the bed. Farley picked it up, remaining sharp-eyed and wary.

"Inspector Bailey of London has offered us $2,500 for you," he said.

"My fee would naturally be commensurately higher," Macdonnell assured him levelly. It never occurred to him that he would not be able to bribe his way out of trouble with the New York police. As the *Tribune* said: "A detective who should refuse to subordinate, for money, the interests of his employer, the people, to the interests of the malefactor he is sent to hunt, would be strangely out of place in the detective force of New York."

"Hurry up with the dough," Detective Farley snarled.

Macdonnell sat down calmly in the gilt armchair and began to rummage through his case.

"Reckon you have quite a pile of gold watches, Inspector?" he asked conversationally. "Maybe you're short on diamond necklaces. Or would you prefer sovereigns?"

"For Christ's sake hurry. We managed to slip aboard without the Deputy Sheriff. He will be raising hell just now. And God knows how long Irving can keep Pinkerton's men off the ship."

Macdonnell looked up slowly, but he did not flinch. Only the tightening of the muscles round his eyes betrayed his feelings.

"Pinkerton's men?" he queried lightly.

"Yes, they were following close behind."

Macdonnell was thinking fast. "Can you smuggle me off the far side of the boat?"

"We dare not," Farley told him. "We are police officers, remember."

Macdonnell stared coldly at the hypocrite, then in one swift movement he turned his case upside down above the bunk. A cascade of bonds and jewelry fell out on to the white sheets and thousands of sovereigns poured over the red coverlet.

"Help yourself," Macdonnell said. He dumped his case on the floor and stepped quickly over to the wardrobe. He pulled out his most expensive suit and hastily began to dress.

"How the hell do I get out of this?" he flung at Farley.

But Farley was preoccupied. His jacket was unbuttoned, he was squeezing packages of bonds into his trouser pockets.

"Don't trouble yourself. I'll take everything incriminating," Farley assured him. "If you take on first-class lawyers you will win a fight against extradition."

Macdonnell turned sharply from the mirror, where his nervous fingers were running into trouble with his collar stud. He stepped forward and his long ringed hand covered the final packet of bonds before Farley reached them.

"I require these for my defense," Macdonnell told him shortly.

Farley turned on Macdonnell a pair of outraged eyes.

"Aw, come on, Mac," he pleaded. "You can trust me. I'll keep them bonds to pay your counsel."

"Mind you don't forget," Macdonnell warned, drawing back his hand. But Farley's hand shot forward and gripped Macdonnell's wrist.

"That's a fine ring you have," he murmured greedily.

There was no answering enthusiasm in Macdonnell's eyes as he stripped off the £400 diamond ring and dropped it into Farley's hand.

Five minutes later Macdonnell was dressed and shaved and Farley was moaning quietly to himself.

"Guess I'll have to leave them sovereigns behind," he grumbled.

Macdonnell's eyes flicked over the detective. He was weighed down like a Spanish donkey. The bed was bare of bonds and most of the hard cash had vanished. All that remained were a pile of sovereigns and a cluster of jewelry.

It was Farley who started guiltily when angry voices sounded along the passage. "Intolerable to be obstructed so long" . . . "a complete misunderstanding" were audible above the rush of feet. The door burst open. Two Pinkerton men came in. They barely glanced at the occupants of the cabin. One crossed to the bed and began to itemize the valuables remaining there while the other pulled out Macdonnell's cabin trunk and started to ferret through it.

Judson Jarvis stormed into the cabin, closely followed by Sheriff Curry and Captain Irving of the New York police. The Bank of England's solicitor in New York drew up behind them, peering at Macdonnell.

Jarvis turned to Farley, who leaned against the bulk-head by the door.

"How dare you scramble on board before me?" he stormed.

Farley evaded the question.

"Meet my prisoner, George Macdonnell," he said. "I formally hand him over to you." Farley smiled grimly. With witnesses all around, he was assured of his $2,500 reward.

"Good morning, gentlemen. What can I do for you?" Macdonnell asked.

"We have a warrant to search your property for anything which may have been fraudulently obtained from the Bank of England," Jarvis told him.

"This is completely ridiculous," Macdonnell drawled. "But pray go ahead and search," he waved his cigar round the room. "There is nothing here which could possibly implicate me in such a crime."

"Stand up. Lift your hands above your head," the Deputy ordered.

He searched Macdonnell and found a gold watch and chain, two uncut diamonds, and a wallet containing five greenbacks. Everyone was turned into the corridor while Pinkerton's men made a thorough search. They pulled the mattress on to the floor and slit open the ticking cover, ripped up the carpet and levered up the floorboards. But no bonds were found. Back in the cabin Jarvis turned hot eyes on Farley.

"This man has stolen a fortune from the Bank of England. Where is it?"

Macdonnell looked outraged. "I must object to that statement, Sheriff. I am a completely innocent man. You can send me back to England on no such charge."

"Search the room again," ordered the Sheriff.

But a second search revealed nothing.

"It's that fellow Farley," the Sheriff exploded. "Where the hell has he got to?"

But the detective had edged down the passage and out of sight.

"Farley found nothing, sir," Captain Irving lied earnestly. "We possessed an attachment against the prisoner only, not against his possessions."

The Bank of England lawyers were not completely stupid. Although they had been unable to prevent the New York City police from gaining an order to arrest Macdonnell, they had refused them any order for his property. Now the lawyer realized his precautions had been in vain.

"It is an outrage," he shouted.

"Macdonnell must have had an accomplice on the boat," Captain Irving decided. "I will order my men to search every suspicious character on board." Irving turned to leave the room, but the attorney stepped forward in his path. He poked a shivering forefinger at Irving.

"It's monstrous," he said. "You will hear more of this, I promise you."

When Farley had dumped his haul he returned along the passage to take charge of Macdonnell. He escorted him to the *Seneca,* which was soon speeding back across the harbor. Reporters watching Macdonnell land on American soil, reported next day:

George Macdonnell has displayed not the slightest nervousness or agitation since the moment of his arrest and conducts himself more like a man against whom some gross outrage was committed than a prisoner charged with that stupendous crime.

Macdonnell was driven to police headquarters and locked up. The next day Mr. J. R. Fellows, Mr. Charles W. Brooke and Mr. J. R. Dos Passos were briefed to defend him against the British Government's demand for extradition. Meanwhile Frances Grey was summoned to New York as witness and left England under police escort.

Seward, Blachford, Griswold and Da Costa, the Bank of England lawyers in New York, hastily drew up an attachment against Inspector Farley and Captain Irving. This was served on them on March 26th, demanding the recovery of any property taken from Macdonnell. The detectives answered that a pistol was all they received. The Bank of England then informed the Commissioner of Police in New York of some very suspicious facts concerning Farley's arrest of Macdonnell on *Thuringia*. The Commissioner blandly replied that the Bank of England might like to prosecute the officers involved. The bank's response was that they had no duty in the matter beyond putting the Commissioner in possession of the facts. Irving and Farley continued to hold positions of trust in the City Police.

20

MOST WANTED MAN
IN EUROPE

In Edinburgh the east wind snarled round the elegant squares, stalked down alleys and hurled itself screaming along wide avenues. Hailstones rattled on to the steep streets and ice made treacherous the many outside stairways of the city.

On the afternoon of March 11th, 1873, George Bidwell stopped outside the green front door of a terraced house. A card announcing "Lodgings to Let" was wedged in the front window. Bidwell climbed the stone steps and rang the brass bell. A flurry of snow buffeted his face and settled on the dustbin lids at the base of the area steps. George Bidwell shivered and glanced uneasily down the street.

With luck his pursuers had been foxed by his doubling back to Scotland, but he could not be sure.

The door of 22 Cumberland Street was opened by a woman of about fifty, who stood quietly in the doorway, omitting the conventional phrases of welcome, and the look from her steady gray eyes was uninquisitive. Bidwell raised his hat wearily.

"Madam, you have a room to let? I am very tired. I arrived from Rotterdam this morning." He spoke in broken English.

Mrs. Laverock continued to survey the crumpled figure on her doorstep. Bidwell's eyes were red-rimmed through lack of sleep, his cheeks blotched with fever.

"I have a room," she answered coolly, but she did not smile.

"Thank you, madam." Bidwell's words were a gasp of relief. "My name is Monsieur Coutant," he said. "I am French."

He lifted his case and eased through the door. And then he heard footsteps on the stairs and men's loud voices.

"Who is that?" he asked sharply.

"They are my lodgers."

"Are they French or German?"

"They are young Scottish gentlemen. Students at the medical school," Mrs. Laverock reassured him.

Bidwell nodded. He followed his landlady down the stone corridor and into her best sitting-room fronting the street. It was a large gaunt room, sparsely furnished, but the bed was soft and the coal fire generously stoked. Mrs. Laverock asked for a week's rent in advance and then withdrew.

Two days' rest in the security of Mrs. Laverock's establishment transformed George Bidwell. All his old assurance returned. It was not so much optimism which colored Bidwell's vision as a reckless determination to succeed. By juggling with the facts he was able to transform his desperate situation and persuade himself he was almost out of danger.

He told himself he could board a transatlantic boat from an unguarded Scottish port, but overlooked the fact that £4 in cash was all he possessed. He sat down to write to Macdonnell, optimistically assuming his friend must be safe home in America.

Edinburgh, March 13th
Dear M,

I think you need have no more anxiety on my account as I feel quite sure of keeping my health intact. I am very quietly and comfortably situated here and shall remain for some days *in status quo*. I shall make a dive for home in one or two weeks longer; of course I have no news of poor Nell, but

I think she will do well for herself and can't imagine on what grounds they hold on. Your friend has had a series of the most extraordinary adventures since you last saw him, a hell's chase and no mistake.

Bidwell addressed the envelope to "Major Matthews, c/o Brevoort House, Fifth Avenue, New York."

Writing to Macdonnell became part of a daily routine. Bidwell breakfasted late in his room and only ventured into the streets at noon. He posted a letter to Macdonnell at the box on the corner and hurried up Dundas Street to a small newsagent's. There he collected the London daily papers, which had to be specially ordered, and return to his lodgings.

The papers were his only contact with the outside world. For hours he rustled through them and afterward burned them. Daily he scanned the personal column of *The Times* for a message from Macdonnell. There were false reports of his own arrest from Liège and Dublin but no information about his colleagues.

Bidwell struggled along Dundas Street against the stabbing sleet. It was Monday morning, March 17th, and it was the worst day of storm since Bidwell had reached Edinburgh a week ago. He turned left down some area steps and wrenched open the door of the newsagent's. The bookseller turned at the sound of Bidwell's footsteps on the wooden floor.

"Good day, Monsieur Coutant, good day." The tall young man hurried forward, his eyes alight with interest. "It was a close thing today. The London papers only arrived a little time ago. The weather is bad all the way to the border. You must be unaccustomed to this in France."

Bidwell's answer was a non-committal grunt. Today he was particularly anxious to collect his papers and get home. They would be bound to carry a report of the third Mansion House examination of Noyes.

"France must be a wonderful country, Monsieur Coutant," the man continued. He had reached the counter, but made no attempt to find the papers.

"Which part of France do you hail from, Monsieur Coutant?"

Bidwell blinked nervously at the Scotsman, who appeared tense with excitement. George realized with a shock that he had unwittingly become the focus of the man's adventurous yearnings and that this could mean danger.

"I don't live in France," Bidwell told him positively. "I live in the Highlands. Now please may I have my papers, I am in a hurry this morning."

"Certainly, sir." The man reached beneath the counter and pulled out Bidwell's thick bundle of papers. George glanced down at them. They were all slightly creased. The bookseller had undoubtedly read them before him.

When Bidwell reached his room he put the papers down on the table. He stripped off his gloves and placed them in the wardrobe drawer. He unbuttoned his overcoat, took off his hat, and hung them on the hatstand. Bidwell picked up the shovel and threw more coal on the fire. He refused to be cowed by a bundle of newspapers. When he was comfortably seated in the leather chair, he picked up *The Times* and turned to the crime page.

"THE GREAT CITY FORGERIES," he read.

Yesterday was appointed for the further examination at the Mansion House of Edwin Noyes, an American, upon the charge of being concerned with another American named Albert F. Warren, and other parties in obtaining nearly £100,000 from the Bank of England by means of the most extraordinary scheme of fraud and forgery, and the proceedings created very great public interest.

There were two other prisoners in custody, one

a fashionably dressed young woman named Ellen Vernon, and a Frenchman named Jules Meunier.

Ellen Vernon was then called as a witness, the prosecuting counsel having intimated that he withdrew the charge against her.

So, they had threatened to prosecute Nellie if she did not betray him.

The Lord Mayor having cautioned her, she expressed her readiness to be examined as a witness. She said—"In August last I became acquainted with an American named George Bidwell."

Next morning Bidwell posted a letter to Macdonnell enclosing a cutting of the Mansion House hearing:

Edinburgh, March 18th
Dear M,
    It made me nearly sick to read what I enclose. I shall try to get hold of Nellie although I may incur some risk by doing so; yet I shall be most cautious in my movements. I am fairly stuck for want of money and cannot put up anything at present, so I shall lie quiet here for a few days and then go to London. Of course I should not have got Nell and myself into this damn stew, who would have dreamed they would take hold of her that way? I look at the Personal in *Times* every day, and in case anyone comes over and does not hit me, a properly worded Personal will do it. You must have $50,000 ready for use for bail if needed.

Bidwell's ready money was disappearing. He had several hundred pounds in diamonds and jewelry but dare not sell them in Edinburgh. If he could get to London there might be a hundred jewelers who would buy the valuables for cash without question.

In the meantime he must arrange to buy his papers elsewhere. The bookseller's behavior had begun to worry him.

The bookseller had grown increasingly suspicious. He had spoken to one of his other customers, who was a clerk in the office of Messrs. Gibson-Craig, Danziel and Brodie, solicitors to the Bank of England in Edinburgh. The clerk was waiting in the shop when Bidwell called for his papers next day and agreed with the bookseller that he resembled the published description of George Bidwell, the wanted forger. The clerk reported his suspicions to his superiors that afternoon.

Nicholson Street, Edinburgh, was a working-class area. Along the row of shabby houses the brass door-knocker of No. 120 shone with unexpected brilliance. At 3 p.m. on March 20th James McKelvie was sitting in the kitchen, polishing his boots to keep himself warm. Suddenly he raised his head and smiled. The rapping of the brass door-knocker was the sweetest sound in the world to James McKelvie, for it meant work.

A uniformed messenger stood outside.

"Are you Private Detective James McKelvie?" he asked.

"Yes."

"Messrs. Gibson-Craig, Danziel and Brodie have an urgent job for you."

"I will come at once."

McKelvie followed the messenger to the premises of the law firm, and was shown into the leading partner's office. The man behind the broad mahogany desk looked up from his papers.

"Detective McKelvie?" he asked briskly. "We want you to find the Bank of England forger."

McKelvie's eyes widened in astonishment. Only in his wildest dreams had he imagined hunting, and finding, the most wanted man in Europe.

"Yes, your honor," he breathed urgently.

The senior partner handed him a file, and briefly

outlined the facts. Mr. Anderson, a bookseller in the city, had grown suspicious of a customer who appeared to be French, said he lived in the Highlands and ordered the London papers every day. He was told to watch the shop and follow the criminal to his hideout.

Dundas Street was a straight, wide road which sloped down to the Water of Leith. It was 11:45 a.m. when McKelvie took up his position ten feet from the area steps leading down to Mr. Anderson's shop.

At noon George Bidwell opened the door of 22 Cumberland Street and walked down the steps to the street. Instead of turning right and then left into Dundas Street, he strode purposefully off in the opposite direction. He crossed Drummond Place and out into Broughton Street where he called at a newsagent to collect the London papers. He returned by the same route. An infallible instinct for self-preservation had caused George Bidwell to change his routine on the very morning danger threatened, and James McKelvie waited in vain.

Having patrolled Dundas Street for three days without seeing anyone answering to Bidwell's description, McKelvie decided that the clerk and the bookseller must have been mistaken. He would not expect a clever criminal, on the run, to indulge in routine habits.

Meanwhile he waited and reached his own conclusions. If the forger had come to Scotland from Ireland he would probably be found in the dockland area where the population was shifting and the transatlantic steamers handy. McKelvie took the train to Glasgow and searched. He returned to Edinburgh and searched. In ten days he found no clue.

In desperation he returned to the bookseller's in Dundas Street and questioned him. Mr. Anderson found an address for M. Coutant in his order book. It was 22 Cumberland Street. Ten minutes later McKelvie was interviewing Mrs. Laverock, and the description she gave of one of her lodgers made McKelvie's heart sing.

He reported to Messrs. Gibson-Craig, Danziel and Brodie that they could expect an arrest immediately and they applied to the City Police for a plain-clothes constable to assist McKelvie.

McKelvie and Constable McNab were watching 22 Cumberland Street when George Bidwell came out of the front door at his usual time on Wednesday, April 2nd. He had been living there quietly for three weeks and was not expecting trouble. He had walked down the steps to the street before he glanced across the road and saw the two men staring at him. Without a pause, Bidwell swiveled round on his heel and returned the way he had come. Locking the door of his room, he ran to the window. Between the net curtains he peered at the two men opposite. He was sure they were detectives. Bidwell turned quickly from the window and pulled out his wallet. It contained two pounds. In his pockets there were two shillings and a foreign coin. He found sixpence in his spare trousers and twopence halfpenny in the stud box. The fare to Glasgow was only a few shillings. He would have to sell some jewelry there. Bidwell pocketed some of the choicest pieces.

If the front door was guarded he must slip out through the back. Cumberland Street was built on a slope and the basement of the house led into the garden, which was surrounded by high stone walls.

He looked about wildly for anything else he might need. He had no gun, so picked up his walking stick from the umbrella stand. Bidwell's eyes narrowed as he gazed through the window. The men had disappeared. He glanced at his watch and waited. Twelve minutes later there was still no sign of the two men. Perhaps his nerves were getting the better of his sense. He swallowed down his anxiety and decided to go out as usual.

By a supreme effort of will Bidwell did not turn round until he reached the corner of Scotland Street where he stopped to post a letter. He stared hard down the street behind him, then moved on to fetch his papers.

It was when he came out of the shop in Broughton Street that he saw them again. They were standing on the pavement on the other side of the road, staring intently at him. Were they uncertain of his identity? If he could throw them off without creating more suspicion, he might catch a cab to the station and be in Glasgow before dark. A heavy wagon rumbled down the street and directly it drew parallel, Bidwell dodged quickly down a side-street on the right. Halfway down Forth Street he turned left into Hart Street and left again. As he completed the square, and came out into Broughton Street again, Bidwell turned his head. The two men were barely four yards behind.

He ran madly down the road. "Stop him, stop him," shouted someone, and Bidwell swerved into a churchyard. Dodging between the gravestones, he noticed there was a wall ahead. It seemed about six foot high. He jettisoned his walking stick and threw himself at the wall, groping and clutching with his hands and feet for a foothold. He was up, and over. He landed in a heap in a flower-bed and found himself in a square patch of garden behind a terraced house. The wall on the left was crumbling and broken. Bidwell hopped over it, ran down the next garden and pulled open the back door of the house. He stepped inside and fumbled his way down a corridor. He opened the front door at the end, slipped through and slammed it behind him. He stopped to regain his breath, listening for footsteps in the house behind. There were none. Thankfully he slumped against the door-jamb. And then he heard a shout. One of the men had turned the corner of the street and was pounding along the pavement toward him. Bidwell started forward, staggered and clutched at the railings. In a moment he was running again. The pounding of his blood filled his head, but his legs kept moving forward. He felt a terrible pain in his side and stumbled. The next thing he knew he was on his knees, his trouser leg drenched in blood. McKelvie's hand was on his shoulder. George Bidwell had been captured. It was a splendid single-handed effort by Private Detective James McKelvie and when Constable McNab finished the course he arrested Bidwell formally. Poor McKelvie contracted typhus fever two months later, and died on 15th June 1873.

21

TRICK
NUMBER THIRTEEN

The barouche turned out of Chambers Street and rattled down Broadway. It was a blazing afternoon in early June. Four of the five men crowded into the carriage were hot and uncomfortable. The fifth member of the party appeared to be enjoying himself immensely. George Macdonnell laughed and talked with his companions, smiling gaily through the window at the large crowd gathered on the sidewalks to see him pass.

Macdonnell smoked a cigar, which he held in his free hand. The other was handcuffed to the wrist of a United States officer, seated on his right. The officer was armed and so were Chief Deputy Marshal Kennedy and Deputies Robinson and Crowley.

After much protracted argument Commissioner Gutman had finally sustained the Bank of England's plea on all points and ordered Macdonnell to be remanded in the custody of United States marshals until he was handed over to the British authorities for extradition.

Macdonnell had scarcely had time to say goodbye to his counsel before being hustled into the carriage. And directly the barouche reached the Battery he was bundled on board the tugboat *Schultz*. The New York papers had reported Macdonnell as being "too sharp to be caught by the wiliest Englishman," and the authorities were taking precautions. To foil any last-minute escape plans the prisoner was to be housed in the iron-balconied prison on Governor's Island.

When the prison clock struck 1 a.m. next morning

Macdonnell climbed out of bed. He had tried to relax and sleep, but it was hopeless. He took a cigar from his case, lit it carefully and picked up the newspaper. Until dawn he pretended to read rather than endure a conversation with his warders. One of these reported his every move next day to a representative of the *New York Herald*.

Macdonnell played out his role in the grim charade next morning. To the perceptive his attitude of cool indifference had begun to appear a little forced. But the large crowd assembled on the wharf were impressed. Macdonnell "walked very leisurely, smoked, laughed and appeared in a state of unaccountable good humor." When he reached the barge he shook hands with the deputies, marshals and sergeants. Then he went aboard and entered into some trivial conversation with the British police, Messrs. Williams, Hancock and Webb. After the detectives had given a receipt for him to Marshal Fiske, Macdonnell was transferred to the *Minnesota*.

On the transatlantic voyage Macdonnell was withdrawn and silent and on the morning of June 18th joined his three accomplices in the Justice Room of the Mansion House. The Lord Mayor, Sir Sydney Waterlow, presided. He had swallowed the impertinence that Bidwell had used his firm to print sundry details connected with the forgeries. Amongst those present on the benches were the Governor and Deputy Governor of the Bank of England, three other directors of the Bank and two members of the House of Rothschild. The inquiry into the forgeries had been the longest on record in the annals of the Lord Mayor's Court, but all the culprits were now assembled in the dock.

Macdonnell watched the proceedings intently. The pace was intolerably slow. A string of witnesses were called, sworn in, and asked for their names and particulars. Sir Harry Poland, greatest criminal lawyer of the age, led each witness through a maze of detail to one vital point. Mr. John Rudolph Lorent came first and proved that a certain bill produced had not been accepted by him, nor by his authority. Mr. Mildmay of Barings, Mr. Tussaud of the Union Bank of London, Mr. Billinghurst of the London and Westminster Bank, each supplied a single fact which added one piece to the gigantic prosecution dossier. The Bank of England solicitors, Messrs. Freshfields, had assembled over a hundred witnesses to testify in these preliminary hearings against the four Americans.

And Noyes had heard them all. Macdonnell glanced along the row at the man who had been called eighteen times to the dockrail and endured four months of solitary confinement in Newgate Prison. The experience had transformed the boyish, carefree face of Edwin Noyes. Now a blank look clouded his eyes. "From first to last," the Lord Mayor later said, "Noyes behaved in a manner entitling him to respect."

George Bidwell was busy writing. Macdonnell watched him pause, glare across the court, and then scribble out another protest on paper thoughtfully provided by the management. Bidwell's resentment against authority had solidified to hate. The smallest error in a witness's statement made him seethe with fury. Leaning forward over the dock-rail, he handed the notes to his counsel, Mr. Metcalfe. The Q.C. read them. "Another case of false identification," Bidwell protested. "Pure fancy and self-glorification." Metcalfe placed them neatly on the pile accumulating on his desk. These details were little aid in building his case for the defense.

A constable had been placed in the dock between the Bidwell brothers to prevent an exchange of notes and conversation which had previously disturbed the proceedings.

The constable's vacant expression made a convenient transition between George's active participation and Austin's polished detachment.

The younger Bidwell had proved a menace in the

courtroom. Disturbing witnesses by idiotic reactions to their words, finding humor where none was intended and acting as if the Lord Mayor's Court of Justice were nothing more impressive than a third-rate music hall.

Austin favored Macdonnell with a falsely innocent, disarming smile. As Macdonnell grinned back, his black mood lifted. He told himself a door would open to save him from disaster. In the meanwhile he would make the best of the somewhat mediocre entertainment offered.

After the hearing Macdonnell was conveyed to Newgate where he was locked into a whitewashed cell, double the length of a coffin. It contained a plank bed with rugs and pillows, a commode, a stool and an iron pail for water. He examined the contents of the single shelf above the bed: a wooden spoon, a tin plate, a gallipot to dring from, a piece of soap, a Bible, a prayer book and a copy of the prison rules. Light seeped in through a heavily barred window at night from a single gas jet.

He further discovered that food was scarce and unpalatable, communication between fellow prisoners forbidden, and all letters censored by the authorities.

How could he improve his situation? Macdonnell studied the warders, who were uniformly underpaid. He soon became acquainted with Sub-Warder Owen Norton, a happy-go-lucky cockney with a wife and six children to support.

For a few shillings weekly Norton willingly arranged for meals to be sent in from Mr. Allwood's eating house. A further bribe, and Norton was passing messages to Austin, George and Noyes. Ultimately he left the prison with letters to America concealed in his clothing and returned on duty with cigars tucked into his socks.

Norton admired Macdonnell. He confided in him that he was saving the extra money to emigrate. Tasmania, it appeared, was the goal of Norton's dreams.

Macdonnell set out a simple plan to solve both their problems. He would be pleased to provide £100 in cash if Norton could contrive to release the four Americans from jail one evening. Once outside the prison, they would all drive straight to Tilbury, and board a ship due to sail with the tide. On arrival in Tasmania, the Americans would further provide capital to launch a joint business venture. It sounded a crazy and unrealistic scheme. But astonishingly there were certain existing factors that made the idea a possibility.

Newgate Jail occupied a unique position, abutting the Central Criminal Court, and its function was to accommodate prisoners awaiting trial. It was not a place of detention for convicts. Prisoners wore their own clothes and security precautions were lax. It had been discovered that unconvicted men rarely gave trouble or tried to escape:

> The non-criminal feel secure in the consciousness of their innocent; the criminal are apt to feel that as soon as the policeman's hand is laid on their shoulders "the game is up" with them. If their courage revives it is mainly for reflections on the glorious uncertainties of the law, and if they have any ready cash they are much more anxious to secure the services of skilled counsel than to waste it on attempts to bribe their jailers.
>
> *Daily Telegraph,* August 26th, 1873.

But after a few days' consideration, Norton decided against Macdonnell's plan. It was too dangerous. Each night three warders were allotted to each three corridors of the prison. Warders Smith and Leach were his mates on the present rota. They would undoubtedly spot any suspicious move he made. Immediately Macdonnell suggested that Norton should procure Smith and Leach for £100 each. Norton approached them and the two men agreed to the scheme, provided they received the cash in advance.

Macdonnell was delighted. He handed over the project to George Bidwell, who immediately perceived that the first essential was to establish a contact outside the prison. He sent to America for his brother John.

In the two-month interval before the case was brought to trial at the August Sessions, Bidwell worked out the details of one of the most fantastic escape plans to be hatched in Newgate Jail.

22

GUNS
IN COURT

George Bidwell took out his handkerchief and wiped his hands, which were damp and clammy. He was unsuitably dressed in the tight-fitting frock-coat he had picked up in the Dublin market many months before. He also wore a six weeks' growth of beard to baffle hostile witnesses.

It was Wednesday, August 20th, and the sun burned down on London. The four Americans were standing in the dock of the Central Criminal Court at the Old Bailey, accused of forgeries on the Governor and Company of the Bank of England amounting to upward of £100,000. They had been charged with no fewer than sixteen serious indictments, to which they had all pleaded not guilty. The prosecution brief ran to a thick volume of 242 pages, with an elaborate index for reference.

Judge Archibald presided. The proceedings had created sensational excitement. There was not a spare seat in the well of the court; Alderman and sheriffs were squeezed together on the benches and the triple-arched public gallery was jammed.

Sir Hardinge Giffard opened the case for the prosecution from his elevated seat beneath the judge's dais. His large square face and stocky build made him look like a prosperous butcher. Giffard considered it superfluous to cultivate a majestic bearing, dramatic gestures or even a well-modulated speaking voice. He preferred to practice the undramatic virtues of accuracy, clarity, moderation and common sense. At fifty Giffard was at the height of his powers, the absolute master of his trade.

He opened by telling the jury they might seek in vain for a parallel to the fraud in the criminal records of the country. He praised the consummate skill with which the prisoners surmounted the difficulties involved in such an ambitious enterprise, and regretted their talents had not been employed in legitimate business.

For upward of three hours he spoke in clear, concise English, explaining the entire working of the fraud, and ended with the statement:

> The jury will say by their verdict, when they have heard the evidence, whether it is possible to entertain the smallest doubt that each and all of the prisoners combined together in carrying out their gigantic scheme. And having, as they thought, destroyed all traces of the proceeds, sought to betake themselves to another country and there enjoy their ill-gotten gains.

Next day the witnesses began to give their evidence. First Mr. Green, the Savile Row tailor, followed by Mr. Fenwick, sub-agent of the Western Branch, then Colonel Francis. Sir Alfred Charles de Rothschild spoke of fraudential bills presented in his name. Charles Norman, of Baring Brothers, Charles Sibeth, of Suse and Sibeth, and six other directors of the leading City banking houses, refuted bills supposed to be accepted by them.

The trial had reached its third day, and it was obvious that the odds were heavily stacked against the four Americans, who listened with marked indifference to the European bankers giving evidence against them.

Austin was almost asleep on his feet. No seats were provided for the prisoners. He leaned his elbow on the dock rail, his palm and splayed fingers supporting his head. His eyes were closed, his mouth half open, small beads of sweat had broken out along his nose. Macdonnell was busy transcribing the proceedings into Greek to keep himself amused.

George Bidwell stared thoughtfully around him, assessing the atmosphere of the courtroom. His eyes swept through the crowded benches reserved for ticket-holders and came to rest on the faces of two men known to him personally.

One man was partially obscured by the giant torso of Big Bill Pinkerton, who had traveled from New York to hear the case. The other, peering from behind Pinkerton's left shoulder, had the same square head as the Bidwells, the same sallow skin, the same air of relentless self-confidence. He was John Bidwell, their brother.

John Bidwell, with a cousin of Macdonnell's, had arrived in England intent on helping their kinsmen prepare their defense, and the sheriffs had generously allotted them seats in court during the trial. The two men had attended the trial every day. They seemed prosperous and mingled easily with the distinguished personalities crowding the reserved seats. Onlookers might consider they held no particular sympathy for the prisoners in the dock. But this was a front. The two men were waiting for a sign. They had waited three days.

Now George Bidwell, from the dock, and John Bidwell, from the well of the court, stared warily at one another. George gave a careful nod of the head. The contact was over in a moment, and both pairs of eyes slid smoothly away in opposite directions.

But a third man had seen the interchange. He was lounging against the dark oak surround to the courtroom wall. As a precaution, the police had detailed a man to watch John Bidwell during court proceedings. The detective drew himself up slowly. A routine job had suddenly become interesting. The man in the dock had passed a message to his brother. What message?

Up in the dock George Bidwell felt suddenly jubilant. The gloom of inertia was dispelled.

The court adjourned at 4 p.m. The judge and aldermen left the dais, and the jury were conveyed by the ushers to a coach placed at their disposal by the Sheriff. The jury were not allowed to separate while the case was pending and the coach took them for an airing through the City before returning them to virtual imprisonment at the Terminus Hotel in Cannon Street.

The court ushers threw open the main doors of the court and John Bidwell breathed the cool air thankfully. He spoke softly to his companion as they filed out of the room.

"We'll be needing that carriage for eleven o'clock tomorrow evening."

Macdonnell's cousin nodded.

"I leave you to make the final bookings at Tilbury," he continued.

"O.K. You can rely on me."

John Bidwell paid a newsboy a penny for a paper. Elbowing through the crowd of curious onlookers, he walked quickly past the prison, and out into Newgate Street. When he crossed the road to the bus-stop it never occurred to him to look behind to see if he was being followed.

Several men were lingering on the pavement waiting for a bus. To make contact easy, John Bidwell stopped amongst them, opened his *Daily Telegraph* and refolded it. He pretended to read the paper with the crime page facing outward. It was headed "THE GREAT CITY FORGERIES."

There was a general movement forward when the clatter of the bus sounded along the street. John Bidwell glanced up. A man was standing at his elbow. Bidwell lifted his top-hat briefly. "Excuse me," he said, repeating the recognition code his brother George had told him, "is this the bus to the Bank of England?"

The man glanced round amongst the other bystanders.

"Yes," he muttered nervously, "I am going there myself."

The detective following Bidwell walked quickly past the bus-stop and turned into a grocer's doorway further down the street. From his vantage point he watched Bidwell swing up on to the platform of the bus. He ran forward and stepped aboard as the horses shook away the flies from round their eyes, and, straining at the traces, dragged the bus away.

John Bidwell was not among the double row of passengers inside the bus. The detective clambered up the curving staircase to the open top deck, where the seats were placed back to back in blocks of four. John Bidwell was sitting halfway along on the outside, facing forward. The seat beside him was occupied by a man wearing the uniform of a Newgate warder. As the man turned to speak to Bidwell the detective recognized the profile of Owen Norton. The detective stiffened. He must be careful. The Newgate warders were on speaking terms with most of the City detectives. Norton would recognize him. He slid forward crabwise and slipped into the seat directly behind Norton, straining to hear the conversation. But Norton and Bidwell were talking quietly and the traffic sounds were thunderous. The rumble of wheels grinding over stone cobbles blurred most of the words, but not all. John Bidwell and Norton were discussing the final moves in the breakout, timed for the next evening. As the bus trundled down through the City and on to the East End, the detective received a fragmentary but convincing impression that an escape was planned.

He followed Bidwell and Norton to the warder's home and watched two other visitors arrive. He recognized them as Newgate warders named Smith and Leach. It was midnight when the detective arrived back at Bow Lane Police Station and made his report.

Next morning lawyers, special visitors and public arriving to attend the forgery case at the Old Bailey found the courtroom doors closed against them. Puzzled, they hung about the passages speculating on the cause of the delay. Late-comers repeated to them the amazing rumor sweeping through the City that there was "a very well-arranged plot to liberate the four Americans either in open court or from the prison itself."

The lobbies and corridors of the Old Bailey were soon buzzing with the wildest speculation. It was said the four Americans planned to leap the dock-rail and rush the doors. The public were further excited by the sounds of general commotion behind the bolted doors of the courtroom.

Sir Thomas White, Sheriff in charge of court proceedings, was taking no chances. Eight well-built policemen were fanned out through the courtroom searching for concealed weapons of every description. A small group of courtroom officials talked excitedly together beneath the dais and halfway down the main aisle White was in conference with Major Bowman, Chief Superintendent of Police. The clerk of the court was searching desperately for the key to a side door that was never used, but always kept open in case of fire. That morning, detectives questioned every person who passed into the courtroom. All Americans were turned away.

Down through the stone viaduct in Newgate Prison eight armed policemen had taken over from the warders. When Smith, Leach and Norton arrived on duty they were taken into custody and searched. Fifty-nine gold sovereigns were found in Leach's pocket. The three men appeared before a special meeting of the Jail Committee of the Court of Aldermen. They were ordered to forfeit their situations and any pay due to them. Norton was sent for trial, and later sentenced to three months' hard labor.

The four Americans were heavily guarded when they entered the courtroom; armed police watched all the exits and patrolled the corridors outside. With a gun in his pocket, Judge Archibald opened the day's proceedings. It is the only recorded instance of a judge carrying firearms in court.

To the disappointment of the spectators the day passed without a shot being fired. The prisoners appeared crushed and subdued as ten witnesses gave their evidence. The escape plan had proved an unqualified failure.

23

GAME, SET AND
FINAL REVENGE

On the fifth day of the trial Ellen Vernon was called for the prosecution. She had made a special effort to look gay, and was dressed in the height of fashion. The ribbons of her straw boater bobbed merrily as she stepped into the witness-box.

Nellie faced the crowded courtroom, took the oath and described the facts of her first meeting with George Bidwell. Counsel passed her a packet of papers for identification. She untied the red string and looked through them. When she realized they were old love letters from George she broke down completely.

When she had recovered, Sir Hardinge Giffard took her through a résumé of her life with the leader of the forgers until her arrest at Euston Station.

In the afternoon Ellen Franklin testified against Noyes and Frances Grey against Macdonnell. Mrs. Austin Bidwell was not called. An English court of law does not permit a wife to testify against her husband.

At her mother's instigation Jane Bidwell wrote coldly to Austin in prison, telling him he had grossly deceived her, and married her under false pretenses. She was young and her life was still before her. She was not prepared to wait for him, but wished to be freed from the bonds of marriage and start again.

Austin could not believe the words at first. On headed prison paper he dashed off this reply:

Mrs. A. B. Bidwell,

Thou worse than Babylonian whore, thou strumpet, false heart and traitor. That night, when lone and diseased, forsaken and starving, you walk to London or Waterloo Bridge, think of the heart great as Caesar's you were false to, and what you left to consume itself to ashes, that heart that loved you and on which you had often lain and sighed out your love.

Oh thou worse than whore, thou traitor heart, may water turn to blood when you drink, scorpions be your pillow. May the grass wither from thy feet, may the woods deny thee a shelter, earth a home, dust a grace, the sun her light, and thy mother as she will welcome thee with a curse and a beating. Then think of me thou false heart one—that never spek to you but to bless you and whose prosperity you reveled in, but deserted in the first breath of adversity.

"Finis" is not written after my name and I will live (a fortune is mine) to make you pray and pray in vain for death.

Thou worse than whore, be a whore with the curses of your

> Husband
> Austin B. Bidwell

Austin read through the scalding document and wrote a brief postscript:

I dare you to show this to anyone, it is too true.

Jane Bidwell had little opportunity for whoring. She was then five months pregnant, almost hysterical with nerves, and living under the strict care of her mother, Mrs. Devereux, at their old lodgings in Oxford Street.

One warm September night Mrs. Devereux and her maid, Catherine Bassett, were woken by screams. Jane

Bidwell was in labor. Mrs. Devereux dressed quickly and went to attend to her daughter while the maid hurried up and down stairs with towels, bowls and boiling water. A girl, two months premature, was born. Mrs. Devereux washed the child, wrapped it in a blanket, and laid it in front of the fire while she cleaned up.

When she peeped in again the baby was in convulsions. At five minutes to midnight on September 29th, 1873, the child died.

Next morning Mrs. Devereux wrapped the rigid little body in newspapers and placed it in a wooden soap box. She put it away in a cupboard and sat down to consider what to do with the corpse. She worried about the problem for three days and eventually decided that the baby was her grandchild and required decent burial.

Mrs. Devereux consulted the Classified Directory at the nearest post office to discover the name of an undertaker. Early on the morning of October 5th she took the wooden box out of the cupboard, tied on the lid securely and addressed the parcel to Josiah Albin, undertaker, Jonathan Street, Lambeth. The maid carried it down the road to the office of the Parcels Delivery Company. She paid sixpence to have the box delivered and signed the company's book with her name and address.

But it is unlawful to bury a corpse without a certificate from a doctor or a midwife and after the undertaker had unwrapped the infant he contacted the police. Detective Mullord visited the Parcels Delivery Office in Regent Street and obtained Catherine Bassett's address. With a uniformed constable he called at Mrs. Devereux's lodgings. They arrested Jane Bidwell for concealment of the birth of her daughter.

The girl was so ill she had to be carried down the stairs. The police placed her under the care of a Dr. Bennett, and she was given a bed in St. Giles Workhouse. On October 15th she was carried into Bow Street and allowed to sit in a chair in dock, when she appeared before Mr. Vaughan, the magistrate. She was remanded for a week.

On October 22nd, Mrs. Devereux and Catherine Bassett were also charged. The three women were given bail and the case was adjourned for the depositions to be read. It was then decided not to proceed to trial.

Meanwhile, on Saturday morning, August 23rd, the prosecution case against the Bank of England forgers had entered its sixth day. The manageress of Macdonnell's hotel in St. James's Place was called. The late James McKelvie's deposition was read over and clerks and chief cashiers from share brokers in the City gave evidence of dealing with the forgers.

One hundred witnesses had already been heard for the prosecution, the case against the forgers had been proved to the most stubborn disbeliever, but proceedings continued. Engravers and printers from Paternoster Row identified parts of the forged bills as their workmanship; a waiter at the Cannon Street Hotel agreed that Noyes was the man he knew as Mr. Horton's clerk. It was toward the end of a long day that Mr. Charles Chabot, a handwriting expert, was called. He gave his professional opinion that Austin's handwriting appeared on every check of C. J. Horton's and also those of F. A. Warren, and then went on to read some letters. One was from Noyes to his brother in which kindly references were made to his father and mother. There was a muffled protest from the dock as Noyes broke down under the strain. He burst into tears which he tried in vain to conceal from the curious eyes of the public, and sobbed like a child at the recital of a passage in which he rejoiced at the prospect of keeping the home together for the family.

Sir Hardinge Giffard rose to say that that concluded the case for the prosecution, and the court was adjourned until the morning.

Next day the courtroom was more packed than usual,

the lobbies were buzzing and crowded with people waiting to hear the evidence for the defense.

But there was none forthcoming. Again Sir Hardinge Giffard rose.

"My learned friends on the other side have informed me they are not about to present any further evidence to the jury. It is therefore my duty to close, with these few remarks, the case I have presented for your decision."

Sir Hardinge contended that it was incredible that people like the prisoners should have tried to taint the whole currency of commerce in the country by their crime. He said he realized the Bank of England had been twitted for being so easily led into the net, and proceeded to give reasons for their credulity. Briefly, he recalled evidence implicating each of the four men in the forgeries, and ended: "I ask the jury to say by their verdict that all the prisoners have been engaged in one common design to commit a crime the magnitude of which is almost unexampled in the history of this country."

During the speech Macdonnell considered the jury. They were all men, seated in two neat rows of half a dozen, in pews beneath the window. They looked faintly bored but human.

One dissension among them would be enough, for a jury's decision must always be unanimous. Macdonnell cudgeled his wits. The jury would think it natural for a prisoner to plead for himself before sentence, but if he should plead for one of the others might not one of them be moved to compassion? It was worth a try. Macdonnell scribbled a note to his Counsel. It was a plea to address the jury in person. After the luncheon recess permission was given for Macdonnell to proceed.

A journalist reported: "The prisoner in question ranged before him a few square pieces of paper, and calmly began his speech."

It was extraordinary to hear the wide vowels of an

Irish Boston accent echoing through the courtroom. The faces of the jurors creased with concentration as they strove to follow the strange pronunciations. Macdonnell told them he was cutting the ground from under his own feet to plead for a friend. The judge leaned forward.

As I understand you to say that what you are now saying cuts away the ground of any defense from under your feet I can only allow you to address yourself on your own behalf and not on behalf of any other person. I don't know to whom you are alluding but each of the prisoners is represented by Counsel, and if you propose to address the jury on behalf of any other person than yourself I cannot allow you.

Macdonnell bowed in acquiescence and continued. He said that Austin had been severely shaken in an accident on the French railway and withdrawn from participation in the frauds. He said that the handwriting expert was mistaken in thinking Austin had signed Warren's and Horton's checks and that large quantities of bonds posted from England, addressed to Austin and discovered at various hotels in New York, were not in fact intended for him or they would have been posted to Mexico.

"My only object," he was saying after twenty minutes, "is to make reparation to a person who has been deceived and imposed upon and had his confidence violated." Macdonnell paused. His startling blue eyes swept the courtroom.

"I have forgotten a very important matter," he told them. "I had intended to say something on behalf of the prisoner Noyes."

"You cannot be allowed to do that," the judge reproached him. "He is defended by counsel."

George Bidwell then addressed the jury. "I had prepared a statement," he admitted blandly. "But after what Mr. Macdonnell has said it would be mere repetition to attempt it. Macdonnell has spoken the truth, the whole truth and nothing but the truth and Noyes only did what he was told."

Counsel for Austin and Noyes gave brief explanations, the judge summed up and the jury withdrew.

The *Daily Telegraph* reported the next day:

Then came the cry for silence as the twelve jurors returned to their places and the prisoners, who had left the dock, were brought in again by a file of stalwart policemen, who stood in a row immediately behind them. "Are you all agreed?" "We are." "How say you—do you find the prisoner, Austin Biron Bidwell, guilty or not guilty?" To this the foreman answers amid the silence of the court, "Guilty." The question was asked concerning each in turn, and the answer comes back promptly in every case. Then the prisoners are told by the judge that they may speak, if they have any reason to urge against the judgment of the law; and Austin Bidwell asks if it would be any use for him to apply for a short postponement of the sentence. "None whatever." He echoes the words "None whatever" with calm despair and then, folding his arms, speaks mournfully of a misspent youth, lost opportunities, neglected or perverted talents.

Austin went on to speak of Colonel Francis.

There is a gentleman in this court whom I have deeply injured, and whose forgiveness I crave. It is Colonel Francis. I hope that, in the course of years when his resentment wears away, he will give me credit for being sincerely sorry for the wrong I have done him. This is the only reparation I can make.

The judge paused for silence, and then spoke. He dwelt briefly on the enormity of the crime and the audacity and skill with which it had been perpetrated.

"It is not the least atrocious part of your crime," he continued, "that you have given a severe blow to the confidence which has been so long maintained in this country. I cannot conceive a worse case of forgery than this, I cannot perceive any reason for mitigating the sentence of penal servitude for life."

There was a gasp of horror in court. Penal servitude for life was a savage sentence to bestow on four young men for an offense against property.

The Americans were led out of the dock and down the stone conduit into Newgate. They turned and embraced one another.

The judge had ordered that the prisoners' watches and clothing should be sold toward repaying the costs of the prosecution. Next morning the men were stripped of their Savile Row suits and silk underwear and supplied with prison clothes; their heads and faces were shaved; they were manacled and driven out of London in separate compartments of a prison omnibus.

But with great tenacity George Bidwell made a vow not to do a day's work for the Queen. When he arrived at Dartmoor Prison, that "great tomb of the living," he went straight to bed in his cell. Next morning he refused to budge.

The warders tried threats and brutal persuasion; the medical officer could find nothing physically wrong; the padre and Governor argued with him, but nothing would make Bidwell walk.

Eight years later, in 1881, the Governor and Medical Officer of Holloway Prison visited Dartmoor and gave this account of Bidwell:

Long disuse of his legs had reduced him almost to a cripple. The muscles were extremely wasted, both hip and knee joints were contracted in a state of semi-flexion, so that he lay doubled up in a bundle. Though he was examined time after time by experts, no one succeeded in discovering any organic disease, or any other cause for his condition, other than his firmly expressed determination never to do a day's work for the British Government—a threat which he ultimately carried out.

Bidwell was sent to a prison hospital and released on 18th July 1887 on the grounds of extreme ill-health and the belief that he had only a few months left to live. He was met in London by his sister and at the dockside in New York by his wife and son.

In America George Bidwell regained his strength and began to work relentlessly for the release of the others. Eventually a massive petition, asking for clemency for Austin, Macdonnell and Noyes, was signed by such prominent people as Joseph Chamberlain, Mark Twain and Harriet Beecher Stowe. It said, with regard to Austin: "A life sentence on a young man twenty-five years of age for an offense against property seems to me very harsh and inconsistent with the better feeling prevailing in our time." The plea for mercy was refused.

Austin Bidwell was eventually released in 1890 after seventeen years behind bars, and Noyes and Macdonnell in 1891.

The men who challenged the formidable Bank of England, and almost got away with it, had paid the penalty for one of the most ingenious frauds of all time.

George Bidwell spent the rest of his life lecturing undergraduates at American universities against the evils of crime and "the pitfalls of the primrose path."

BIBLIOGRAPHY

Bidwell's Travels from Wall Street to London Prison (or Newgate) or Forging His Own Chains, George and Austin Bidwell, Bidwell Publishing Co., 1897, Hartford, Conn.

Victorian Vista, James Laver, Hulton Press 1954, London

The Victorian Sunset, E. W. Stratford, George Routledge & Co. 1932, London

Victorian Panorama, Peter Quennell, B. T. Batsford 1937, London

The Tichborne Claimant, Michael Gilbert, Hollis and Carter 1957, London

The Memoirs of E. V. Kenealy, Arabella Kenealy, John Long 1908, London

Life of Gladstone, 3 vols., John Morley, Macmillan 1903, London

Disraeli, André Maurois, John Lane 1907, London

William Morris, E. P. Thompson, Lawrence and Wishart 1955

London in the Sixties, One of the Old Brigade, Everett & Co. 1893

Murray's Modern London 1874, John Murray

Dramatic Days at the Old Bailey, Charles Kingston, Stanley Paul and Co. Ltd., London 1923

Mysteries of Police and Crime Vol. 3, Major Arthur Griffiths, Cassell & Co. Ltd., London

Famous Trial Series: The Bank of England Forgery,

edited by George Dilnot, Geoffrey Bles, London 1929

The Bank of England from Within, W. Marston Acres, Oxford University Press, London 1931

London Old and New, Thornbury and Walford, Cassels, London

Londres et ses Environs, Louis Rousselet, Librarie Hachette et Cie, Paris 1874

The Rothschilds, Frederick Morton, Secker and Warburg, London 1961

A Generation of Judges, their Reporter, Sampson Low, London 1886

72 Years at the Bar, Ernest Bowen, Macmillan and Co., London 1924

England Without and Within, Richard Grant White, Sampson and Low, London 1881

Our Railways, 2 vols., John Pendleton, Cassell 1894

Cuba with Pen and Pencil, S. Hazard, Sampson Low 1873

Ireland, J. N. Murphy, Longmans Green 1870

The Pearl of the Antilles, A. Gallenger, Chapman & Hall 1873

Principal Sources

Transcript of the trial from Somerset House
Files of *The Times, Daily Telegraph, Evening Standard, New York Herald Tribune, Cork Examiner, Irish Times, Echo, City Press, Illustrated London News* and *Punch.*

INDEX